CONTENTS

O9-BTO-438

Passive Voice ∎

This Is a Very Good Photograph of You

George took this photograph.
This photograph **was taken** by George.

A. This is a very good photograph of you.
B. I think so, too.
A. Who **took** it?
B. I'm not sure. I think it **was taken** by my Uncle George.

A. This is a sad poem.
B. I think so, too.
A. Who **wrote** it?
B. I'm not sure. I think it **was written** by Shakespeare.

1. This is a very cute photograph of your children.
take

2. This is an excellent magazine article.
write

3. This is a beautiful sonata.
   compose

4. This is really an exciting movie.
   direct

5. This is a very funny political cartoon.
   draw

6. This is a very fine portrait of you.
   paint

7. This is a very useful machine.
   invent

8. This is an impressive bridge.
   build

9. This is a magnificent building.
   design

10. This is a very talented elephant.
    train

11. This is a very strange computer.
    program

12. This is really a crazy fad.
    begin

3

He's Already Been Fed

Somebody has fed the dog.
The dog **has been fed**.

Somebody has turned off the lights.
The lights **have been turned off**.

A. Do you want me to feed Rover?

B. No. Don't worry about it. He's already **been fed.**

A. Do you want me to ring* the church bells?

B. No. Don't worry about it. They've already **been rung**.

*ring–rang–rung

1. *make the bed*

2. *send the packages*

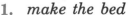

3. *do the dishes*

4. *sweep the porch*

5. *carve the turkey*

6. *hide* the Christmas presents*

7. *write down Mary's telephone number*

8. *freeze† the leftover chicken*

9. *take the garbage out*

10. *wake** the children up*

11. *teach two word verbs today*

12. *sing the National Anthem*

*hide–hid–hidden
†freeze–froze–frozen
**wake–woke–woken

Have You Heard About...?

A. Have you heard about Harry?
B. No, I haven't. What happened?
A. He **was fired** last week.
B. What a shame!* That's the second time he's **been fired** this year!

A. Have you heard about Helen?
B. No, I haven't. What happened?
A. She **was given** a raise last week.
B. That's great!† That's the second time she's **been given** a raise this year!

*Or: That's terrible! That's too bad!
†Or: That's fantastic! That's wonderful!

1. *Mr. and Mrs. Wilson*
   robbed

2. *Uncle John*
   invited to the White House

3. *Larry*
   hurt in a car accident

4. *Maria*
   promoted

5. *our mailman*
   bitten* by a dog

6. *the man across the street*
   arrested

7. *Claudia*
   sent to Honolulu on business

8. *Mrs. Miller*
   taken to the hospital by ambulance

9. *Arthur*
   rejected by the army

10. *Lana*
    offered a movie contract

11. *Walter*
    chosen† "employee of the month"

12.

*bite–bit–bitten
†choose–chose–chosen

7

ALAN ALMOST DIDN'T GET TO WORK THIS MORNING

Alan almost didn't get to work this morning.

As he was leaving his apartment building, he was hit on the head with a flowerpot which had been put on a windowsill by one of his neighbors.

As he was walking to the bus stop, he was bitten by a dog and stung by a bee.

While he was waiting for the bus, he was almost run over by a car.

While he was riding on the bus, his wallet was stolen. All his money and identification cards were taken.

As he was walking into his office building, he was accidentally knocked down by a boy delivering newspapers.

And when Alan finally got to work, he was yelled at by his boss for being an hour late.

Poor Alan! What a way to begin the day!

CHECK-UP

True, False, or Maybe?

Answer True, False, or Maybe (if the answer isn't in the story).

1. As Alan was leaving his apartment building, one of his neighbors hit him on the head.
2. As he was walking to the bus stop, a dog bit him and a bee stung him.
3. A car almost hit Alan.
4. Alan had a lot of money in his wallet.
5. Alan accidentally knocked down a boy delivering newspapers.
6. Alan was yelled at because he wasn't on time for work.

How about YOU?

Have you ever had a bad day when everything went wrong? What happened? When? How did you feel?

A VERY EXCITING YEAR

In January Martha was hired by the Fernwood Company as a secretary. In March she was sent to school by the company to study statistics and accounting. In April she was given a raise. Just two months later, she was promoted to the position of supervisor of her department.

In August she was chosen "Employee of the Month." In October she was given another raise. In November she was invited to apply for a position in the company's overseas office in Bangkok. And in December she was given the new job and flown to Thailand to begin work.

Martha certainly has had a very exciting year. She can't believe all the wonderful things that have happened to her since she was hired just twelve months ago.

✔ CHECK-UP

Choose

1. The interviewer liked my resume, so I was given the ____.
   a. raise
   b. position

2. After Ted had worked at the company for two years, he was ____.
   a. promoted
   b. hired

3. I was sent overseas ____ my company.
   a. by
   b. as

4. Over one hundred people have ____ the new position.
   a. been invited to
   b. applied for

5. Last month Sarah was ____ a new position in the Accounting Department.
   a. chosen
   b. given

6. I have to type this myself. The new secretary hasn't been ____ yet.
   a. hired
   b. fired

Tell about things that have happened in your life during the past twelve months.

9

It's Being Repaired Right Now

Somebody is repairing my car.
My car is **being repaired**.

A. Hello. Is this Joe's Auto Repair Shop?

B. Yes, it is. Can I help you?

A. Yes, please. This is Mrs. Jones. I'm calling about my car. Has it **been repaired** yet?

B. Not yet. It's **being repaired** right now.

A. I see. Tell me, when can I pick it up?

B. Come by at four o'clock. I'm sure it'll be ready by then.

A. Hello. Is this _____'s _____?

B. Yes, it is. Can I help you?

A. Yes, please. This is _____. I'm calling about my _____. (Has it/Have they) been _____ yet?

B. Not yet. (It's/They're) being _____ right now.

A. I see. Tell me, when can I pick (it/them) up?

B. Come by at _____ o'clock. I'm sure (it'll/they'll) be ready by then.

1. *watch*
   repair

2. *TV*
   fix

3. *pants*
   take in

4. *poodle*
   clip

5. *will*
   rewrite

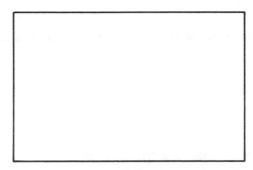

6.

JOE'S AUTO REPAIR SHOP

Wilma Jones has been having a lot of trouble with her car recently, so she decided to take it to Joe's Auto Repair Shop to be fixed. The car is there now and is receiving a LOT of attention from Joe and the other mechanics at his shop.

The engine is being tuned. The oil is being changed. The battery is being charged. The brakes are being adjusted. The heater is being repaired. The broken headlight is being replaced. The hood is being repainted. The tires are being checked. And the broken rear window is being fixed.

Wilma is aware that she's probably going to be charged a lot of money for these repairs. But she's confident that her car will be returned to her in excellent condition by the fine people who work at Joe's Auto Repair Shop.

✔CHECK-UP

Q & A

Wilma Jones is calling Joe's Auto Repair Shop to find out about her car. Using this model, make questions and answers based on the story.

A. Have you *tuned the engine* yet?
B. No, not yet. *It's* being *tuned* right now.

Listening

Listen and choose the best line to continue the conversation.

1. a. Do you want me to do them?
   b. Who did them?

2. a. Do you want me to send them?
   b. Who sent them?

3. a. Was your cat hurt badly?
   b. Was your dog hurt badly?

4. a. Is she going to go?
   b. Is he going to go?

5. a. When will Mrs. Brown begin working?
   b. When will Mr. Simon begin working?

6. a. When will Mrs. Davis start her new job?
   b. When will Mrs. Clark start her new job?

7. a. Oh, good. I'll pick it up in an hour.
   b. Oh, good. Call me when it's been fixed.

8. a. Oh, good. I'll pick it up right now.
   b. Oh, good. I'll pick it up when it's ready.

A NATIONAL HISTORIC LANDMARK

This building is the original headquarters of the Lord and Lady Department Store Company. It was designed by the famous architect Archibald Morgan. It was built by the Vanderpool Construction Company. Construction was begun in 1845 and was completed in 1847. The building was officially opened in ceremonies that were held on April 13, 1847. These ceremonies were attended by the mayors of several cities, the governor, and the vice-president of the United States.

The building's interior was destroyed by a fire which broke out in the early hours of the morning of February 3, 1895. After the fire, the building wasn't used for several years.

During World War I the structure was used as a warehouse for clothing and other materials which were sent to our soldiers overseas. After the war, the interior was rebuilt. Electric lights and modern plumbing were installed, and the Lord and Lady Department Store was officially reopened on June 17, 1921.

Since its opening day, the Lord and Lady Department Store has been considered one of the finest examples of nineteenth-century American architecture. The store has been visited by the presidents and prime-ministers of many countries.

On December 5, 1973, this building was officially registered as a U.S. National Historic Landmark.

Answer These Questions

1. Who was the building designed by?
2. Who was the building built by?
3. When was construction begun?
4. When was it completed?
5. When was the building officially opened?
6. Who were the opening ceremonies attended by?
7. What happened on February 3, 1895?

8. What was the building used for during World War I?
9. When was the interior rebuilt?
10. When was the building reopened?
11. Since its opening day, what has the building been considered?
12. What happened on December 5, 1973?

Choose

1. The telephone was ____ in my new apartment this afternoon.
   a. opened
   b. installed

2. Our anniversary party was ____ by all of our friends.
   a. attended
   b. visited

3. The shoe factory downtown was ____ by the fire.
   a. rebuilt
   b. destroyed

4. The construction has been completed, and now the department store can be ____.
   a. rebuilt
   b. reopened

5. Our City Hall is ____ by many tourists because it's a very historic building.
   a. visited
   b. registered

6. Our wedding ceremony wasn't ____ outside because it rained.
   a. considered
   b. held

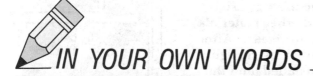

IN YOUR OWN WORDS

For Writing and Discussion

Tell a story about the history of the place where you were born or a place where you have lived. You might want to use some of the following words in your story:

attacked	discovered
begun	founded
built	invaded
captured	liberated
closed	opened
conquered	rebuilt
destroyed	settled

ON YOUR OWN: What's Your Opinion?

> Answers **should be written** in your notebook.
> Students **should be required** to take an examination.
> Smoking **shouldn't be allowed** in public buildings.

Talk about these issues with other students.

1. **Should** your native language **be spoken** during English class?

2. **Should** students **be allowed** to use dictionaries during the lesson?

3. When **should** young people **be allowed** to
   drive?
   drink?
   vote?
   go out on dates by themselves?

4. **Should** smoking **be permitted** in public buildings?

5. **Should** everybody (men and women) **be required** to serve in the army?

GRAMMAR

Passive Voice

This photograph **was taken** by George.
He **was fired** last week.
The lights **have been** turned off.

My car **is being repaired.**

Students should **be required** to take an examination.
Smoking shouldn't **be allowed** in public buildings.

FUNCTIONS

Asking for and Reporting Information

Who *took it*?

What happened?

When?
When can I *pick it up*?

How did you feel?

Have you *tuned the engine* yet?
Not yet. *It's* being *tuned* right now.

Has *it* been repaired yet?
Not yet. *It's* being *repaired* right now.

Have you ever *had a bad day when everything went wrong*?

Have you heard about *Harry*?

Tell me, _____?

I think *it was taken by my Uncle George*.

I'm calling about *my car*.

He's already been *fed*.

Responding to Information

That's great!
That's fantastic!
That's wonderful!

Sympathizing

What a shame!
That's terrible!
That's too bad!

Inquiring about an Opinion

Should *students be allowed to use dictionaries*?

Expressing an Opinion

This is *a very sad poem*.

Students should *be required to take an examination.*
Smoking shouldn't *be allowed in public buildings.*

Expressing Agreement

I think so, too.

Greeting People

Hello. Is this *Joe's Auto Repair Shop*?
Yes, it is.

Offering to Help

Can I help you?

Offering to Do Something

Do you want me to *feed Rover*?

Expressing Certainty

I'm sure *it'll be ready by then*.

Expressing Uncertainty

I'm not sure.

Complimenting

This is a very good *photograph of you*.

Indicating Understanding

I see.

Noun/Adjective/Adverb Review:

Count/Non-Count Nouns ■
Comparative of Adjectives ■
Superlative of Adjectives ■
Comparative of Adverbs ■

Could I Possibly Borrow Some Paper Clips?

many a few	much a little
paper clips eggs mushrooms	sugar paper toothpaste

A. Could I possibly borrow some paper clips?*

B. Sure. **How many** do you need?

A. Just **a few**.

B. Here! Take **as many as** you want!

A. Thanks.

B. You're welcome.

A. Could I possibly borrow some sugar?*

B. Sure. **How much** do you need?

A. Just **a little**.

B. Here! Take **as much as** you want!

A. Thanks.

B. You're welcome.

*Or: Could you possibly lend me some paper clips/sugar?
   Could you possibly spare some paper clips/sugar?

1. *rubber bands*

2. *typing paper*

3. *eggs*

4. *shampoo*

5. *flour*

6. *envelopes*

7. *ink*

8. *mushrooms*

9. *laundry detergent*

10. *toothpaste*

11. *one-dollar bills*

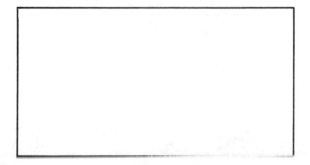

12.

I Need Some Advice

cheap – cheaper	interesting – more interesting
nice – nicer	beautiful – more beautiful
big – bigger	honest – more honest
friendly – friendlier	reliable – more reliable

A. I need some advice. Should I buy a used car or a new car?

B. Hmm. That's a difficult question. Used cars are CHEAPER than new cars.

A. That's true.

B. On the other hand, new cars are MORE RELIABLE than used cars. I really don't know what to tell you.

friendly   clean

1. *buy a dog or a cat*

intelligent   nice

2. *go out on a date with Ted or Ronald*

20

interesting   patient

3. *study English with Ms. Jones or Mrs. Green*

4. *buy ice cream or yogurt for dessert this evening*

convenient   cheap

5. *go to the supermarket across the street or the supermarket around the corner*

fast   safe

6. *buy a motorcycle or a bicycle*

capable   energetic

7. *hire Mr. Clark or Mr. Davis*

TIMOTHY WHITE honest   EDWARD PRATT experienced

8. *vote for Timothy White or Edward Pratt*

exciting   romantic

9. *take my girlfriend to a night club or a cafe tonight*

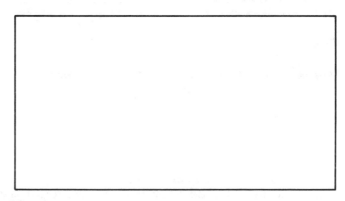

10.

READING

A MEMO FROM THE BOSS

INTEROFFICE MEMORANDUM

To: All Personnel
From: Mr. Davis
Subject: Use of Office Supplies

I'm very concerned about the use of office supplies. During the past year we have been using too many paper clips, too much paper, too many rubber bands, too much ink, too much typing paper, too many envelopes, and too many pens and pencils.

Beginning immediately, I'd like all of you to use fewer paper clips, less paper, fewer rubber bands, less ink, less typing paper, fewer envelopes, and fewer pens and pencils.

Thank you for your cooperation.

 CHECK-UP

Q & A

You're an employee in this office. Mr. Davis is talking with you about your use of office supplies. Using this model, create dialogs based on the memo above.

A. *Howard?*
B. Yes, Mr. Davis?
A. *How many paper clips* have you used today?
B. Not *too many* . . . just *a few*.
A. Good. We've been using *too many paper clips* in this office lately.
B. I know. I read your memo. We're all trying to use *fewer paper clips* these days.
A. Good. I'm glad to hear that. Thank you, *Howard*.
B. You're welcome, Mr. Davis.

BETTER THAN BEFORE

Ronald recently completed a public-speaking class, and he's very pleased with the results. His family has noticed that he's speaking louder, more clearly, and more confidently than before. His boss has noticed that he's more effective in his work. All his friends tell him that he's friendlier and more outgoing than before. And Ronald himself has noticed that he's more comfortable when he speaks with people and he's even enjoying himself more at parties. Ronald is feeling much better about himself these days. That's why he's now recommending the public-speaking class to everybody he knows.

Mr. and Mrs. Peterson recently completed an aerobics class, and they're very pleased with the results. Their children have noticed that they're happier than before. Their friends have noticed that they're looking slimmer and more physically fit than before. All their neighbors tell them that they're more relaxed than before. And Mr. and Mrs. Peterson themselves have noticed that they're more energetic than before. Mr. and Mrs. Peterson are feeling much better about themselves these days. That's why they're now recommending the aerobics class to everybody they know.

Fido recently completed a dog obedience class, and he's very pleased with the results. The other dogs in the neighborhood have noticed that he looks much healthier and prouder than before. The mailman has noticed that he runs faster and jumps higher than before. His family tells him that he rolls over, "plays dead," and does other tricks better than before. And Fido himself has noticed that he feels stronger and looks more handsome than before. Fido is feeling much better about himself these days. That's why he's now recommending the dog obedience class to everybody he knows.

 CHECK-UP

True or False?

1. Ronald is studying public speaking now.
2. Ronald used to speak softer.
3. Mr. and Mrs. Peterson were heavier before.
4. They aren't as energetic as they used to be.
5. Fido didn't do tricks before.

Listening

Listen and choose what the people are talking about.

1. a. public speaking class b. yoga class
2. a. the mailman b. the dog
3. a. bicycles b. employees
4. a. paper b. rubber bands
5. a. a garden b. a cake

How Do You Like Your New Apartment?

warm	–	warmer	– the warmest
friendly	–	friendlier	– the friendliest
nice	–	nicer	– the nicest
big	–	bigger	– the biggest
interesting	–	more interesting	– the most interesting
comfortable	–	more comfortable	– the most comfortable
patient	–	more patient	– the most patient

A. How do you like your new apartment?

B. I like it very much. It's really **big**.

A. Is it **bigger** than your old apartment?

B. It sure is! It's **the biggest** apartment I've ever had.

A. How do you like your new English teacher?

B. I like him very much. He's really **patient**.

A. Is he **more patient** than your old English teacher?

B. He sure is! He's **the most patient** English teacher I've ever had.

1. *winter coat*
   warm

2. *dance teacher*
   talented

3. boss
   nice

4. job
   interesting

5. armchair
   comfortable

6. bicycle
   fast

7. briefcase
   sturdy

8. vacuum cleaner
   powerful

9. dentist
   good*

10. roommate
    considerate

11. parrot
    talkative

12.

*good–better–best

You're Just Saying That!

gracefully – more gracefully
accurately – more accurately
carefully – more carefully

fast – faster
_____
well – better

A. I think I'm getting old.

B. Why do you say that?

A. I don't **dance** as **gracefully** as I used to.

B. That's not true! You **dance more gracefully** than anybody I know.

A. You're just saying that!

B. No! I really mean it!

1. *drive*
carefully

2. *type*
accurately

26

3. *sing*
   beautifully

4. *write*
   neatly

5. *play tennis*
   well

6. *jog*
   fast

7. *think*
   clearly

8. *work*
   energetically

9. *play baseball*
   well

10. *look at life*
    enthusiastically

11. *speak Russian*
    fluently

12.

ON YOUR OWN: TV Commercials

Practice this commercial.

A. I've been worried about my **kitchen floor** recently.

B. Really? What's the matter with your **kitchen floor**?

A. It isn't **shiny** enough, and I don't know how to make it **shinier**. Do you have any ideas?

B. Yes, I do. Have you ever tried PRESTO Floor Wax?

A. No, I haven't. Does it make **kitchen floors shinier**?

B. It sure does! I remember when I was worried about MY **kitchen floor**. It wasn't as **shiny** as I wanted it to be. But one day somebody told me about PRESTO Floor Wax. I started using it, and now everybody tells me I have **the shiniest kitchen floor** in town!

A. Thanks for the advice. I think I'll go to a store and get some right away.

B. You won't regret it.

Using the script above as a guide, prepare commercials for these products.

1. *windows*
   clean

2. *hair*
   attractive

3. *teeth*
   white

4.

28

THE SEASIDE RESORT HOTEL

Shirley and Joe took a vacation last month at the Seaside Resort Hotel. They were very pleased with the hotel and had a wonderful time on their vacation.

The beach was the cleanest and most beautiful they had ever seen. The ocean water was the clearest and warmest they had ever swum in. Their room was the most spacious and most comfortable they had ever stayed in. The food was the most delicious they had ever eaten. The hotel staff was the friendliest and most helpful they had ever encountered. The golf course was the most challenging they had ever played on. And the nightclub show was the most entertaining they had ever been to.

Shirley and Joe really enjoyed themselves at the Seaside Resort Hotel. It was the best vacation they had ever taken.

IN YOUR OWN WORDS

For Writing and Discussion

THE MOUNTAIN VIEW RESORT HOTEL

You took a vacation recently at the Mountain View Resort Hotel, and you had a wonderful time! Using the story above as a guide, tell about your vacation.

GRAMMAR

Count/Non-Count Nouns

How much	sugar paper toothpaste	do you need?		Just	a little.
How many	paper clips eggs mushrooms				a few.

Comparative of Adjectives

Motorcycles are	faster bigger	than bicycles.
	more exciting more interesting	

Superlative of Adjectives

This is	the warmest the nicest	coat I've ever had.
	the most comfortable the most expensive	

Comparative of Adverbs

You dance	more gracefully more beautifully	than anybody I know.
	faster better	

FUNCTIONS

Requesting

Could I possibly borrow
Could you possibly lend me }
Could you possibly spare
 some paper clips?

Responding to Requests

Sure.

Inquiring about Want-Desire

How many do you need?
How much do you need?

Asking for Advice

I need some advice.

Should I *buy a used car* or *a new car?*

Do you have any ideas?

Offering Advice

I really don't know what to tell you.

You won't regret it.

Responding to Advice

Thanks for the advice.

Inquiring about Satisfaction

How do you like *your new apartment?*

Expressing Satisfaction

I like it very much.

Expressing Dissatisfaction

It isn't *shiny* enough.

It wasn't as *shiny* as I wanted it to be.

Describing

It's really *big.*
He's really *patient.*

It's the *biggest apartment I've ever had.*
He's the *most patient English teacher I've ever had.*

Asking for and Reporting Information

How many *paper clips have you used today?*

Why do you say that?

What's the matter with *your kitchen floor?*

Everybody tells me *I have the shiniest kitchen floor in town.*

Responding to Information

Good.

I'm glad to hear that.

Indicating Understanding

I know.

Expressing Inability

I don't *dance* as *gracefully* as I used to.

Expressing Agreement

That's true.

Expressing Disagreement

That's not true!

Complimenting

You *dance* more *gracefully* than anyone I know.

Embedded Questions

I Don't Know Where the Money Is

Where is the bank? | I don't know where the bank is.
What is he doing? | I don't know what he's doing.
Why were they crying? | I don't know why they were crying.
When can he visit us? | I don't know when he can visit us.

A. Where is the money?

B. I don't know where the money is.

Ask and answer these questions, using one of the following expressions in your answer:

I don't know..., I don't remember..., I can't remember...,
I've forgotten..., I'm not sure..., I have no idea...

1. Where are my keys?

2. What was his license number?

3. What are they arguing about?

4. When will the train arrive?

5. Who should I call?

6. Who was the eleventh president of the United States?

7. How long have Mr. and Mrs. Appleton been married?

8. How long has Alan been working here?

9. When is Santa Claus going to come?

I Don't Know What He Looks Like

Where does he live?
How often do they come here?
How did she break her leg?

I don't know where he lives.
I don't know how often they come here.
I don't know how she broke her leg.

A. What does the bank robber look like?

B. I don't know what he looks like.

I don't know..., I don't remember..., I can't remember...,
I've forgotten..., I'm not sure..., I have no idea...

1. Where did you buy your winter coat?

2. How much do eggs cost this week?

3. How often does the ice cream truck come by?

4. What time does the movie begin?

5. When did Mom and Dad get married?

6. What did we do in English class yesterday?

7. Why do young people like such loud music?

8. When did you decide to become a teacher?

9. How much does a haircut cost these days?

33

Do You Know What Time the Concert Begins?

Where is the bank?	
Do you know Can you tell me Could you tell me Could you please tell me Could you possibly tell me Do you have any idea Do you by any chance know	where the bank is?

A. Do you know what time the concert begins?

B. I'm sorry. I don't know. You should ask the man at the box office. HE can tell you what time the concert begins.

A. Can you tell me how long I've been here?

B. I'm sorry. I don't know. You should ask your nurse. SHE can tell you how long you've been here.

1. *Do you know...?*
   ask the ticket agent

2. *Do you by any chance know...?*
   ask the people next door

3. *Could you please tell me…?*
   ask the teacher

4. *Do you by any chance know…?*
   talk to the salesman

5. *Can you tell me…?*
   check with the mechanic

6. *Do you know…?*
   call her friend Patty

7. *Can you tell me…?*
   ask your older brother

8. *Do you know…?*
   ask that police officer over there

9. *Do you have any idea…?*
   call the superintendent

10. *Do you know…?*
    ask his supervisor

11. *Do you by any chance know…?*
    ask the boss

12.

ROSEMARY SMITH WAS ROBBED

Rosemary Smith was robbed about an hour ago while she was walking home from work. She's at the police station now, and she's having a lot of trouble giving the police information. She knows that a man robbed her about an hour ago, but she simply can't remember any of the details.

She has forgotten how tall the man was. She isn't sure how heavy he was. She can't remember what color hair he had. She has no idea what color eyes he had. She doesn't remember what he was wearing. She doesn't know what kind of car he was driving. She can't remember what color the car was. She has no idea what the license number was. And she doesn't even know how much money was taken!

Poor Rosemary! The police want to help her, but she can't remember any of the details.

CHECK-UP

Q & A

You're a police officer. You're trying to get information from Rosemary Smith about the robbery. Using this model, make questions and answers based on the story.

A. Can you tell me* *how tall the man was*?

B. I'm sorry. *I've forgotten how tall he was.*

> *Or: Do you know...?
> Could you tell me...?
> Could you please tell me...?
> Could you possibly tell me...?
> Do you have any idea...?
> Do you by any chance know...?

Choose

1. I'm not sure _____.
   a. where do you live
   b. where you live

2. They don't know _____.
   a. where the museum is
   b. where is the museum

3. Do you remember _____?
   a. where you put the car keys
   b. where did you put the car keys

4. Could you tell me _____?
   a. why Fred was fired
   b. why was Fred fired

5. I have no idea _____.
   a. how much a concert ticket costs
   b. how much does a concert ticket cost

A "SURPRISE" QUIZ

Mrs. Murphy is giving her students a "surprise" history quiz today, and Jeffrey isn't very happy about it. He has been absent for the past several days, and he's having a lot of trouble answering the questions.

He doesn't know who the nineteenth president of the United States was. He isn't sure when the Civil War ended. He doesn't remember when California became a state. He has forgotten where George Washington was born. He can't remember how many people signed the Declaration of Independence. He doesn't know where Abraham Lincoln was assassinated. He has forgotten why Washington, D.C. was chosen as the capital. And he has no idea what Alexander Graham Bell invented!

Jeffrey is very upset. He's sure he's going to fail Mrs. Murphy's "surprise" history quiz.

 *CHECK-UP*

Q & A

The history quiz is over, and Mrs. Murphy is going over the answers with her students. Using the story as a guide, complete the following conversation.

A. Who knows who the nineteenth president of the United States was?
B. I do. It was Rutherford B. Hayes.
A. And who can tell me _____?
C. I can. It ended in 1865.
A. Does anyone know _____?
D. Yes. It became a state in 1850.
A. Who remembers _____?
E. I remember. He was born in Virginia.
A. Can anybody tell me _____?
F. Yes. It was signed by 56 people.
A. Who knows _____?
G. He was assassinated at Ford's Theater in Washington, D.C.
A. And who can tell me _____?
H. It was chosen because the northern and southern states agreed it was a good location for the capital.
A. And finally, who remembers _____?
I. I do. He invented the telephone.
A. Very good, class!

Do You Know if Honey Is Bad for My Teeth?

Is Tom in school today?	Do you know	if / whether	Tom is in school today?
	I don't know	if / whether	Tom is in school today.
Does Mary work here?	Do you know	if / whether	Mary works here?
	I don't know	if / whether	Mary works here.

A. Do you know { if / whether } honey is bad for my teeth?

B. I'm not really sure. Why don't you ask your dentist?

HE can tell you { if / whether } honey is bad for your teeth.

A. Can you tell me { if / whether } anybody here found a black wallet?

B. I'm not really sure. Why don't you ask the manager?

SHE can tell you { if / whether } anybody here found a black wallet.

1. *Can you tell me...?*
   ask Dr. Bell

2. *Do you know...?*
   speak to the stewardess

3. *Could you possibly tell me...?*
   check with the ticket agent

4. *Do you by any chance know...?*
   ask Mr. Parker

5. *Could you please tell me...?*
   ask the bus driver

6. *Can you tell me...?*
   ask the librarian

7. *Do you know...?*
   ask the music teacher

8. *Do you know...?*
   call Mr. Hooper, the landlord

9. *Can you tell me...?*
   ask those people over there

10.

READING

AT THE MIDTOWN MEDICAL CLINIC

It's a busy afternoon at the Midtown Medical Clinic. Lots of people are sitting in the waiting room and thinking about the questions they're going to ask the doctor.

Frank wants to know if he broke his arm. Mrs. Wilkins needs to know if she has lost too much weight. Arnold wants to find out whether he should go on a diet. Mrs. Parker is wondering whether her children have the measles. Dan is hoping to find out if he'll be able to play in the soccer match next week. Linda is going to ask the doctor whether she has to have her tonsils taken out. Edward expects to find out whether he needs glasses. And Vicki is anxious to know if she's pregnant.

Everybody is waiting patiently, but they hope they don't have to wait too long. They're all anxious to hear the answers to their questions.

 CHECK-UP

Q & A

The people in the story are registering with the receptionist at the Midtown Medical Clinic. Using this model, create dialogs based on the story.

A. I'd like to see the doctor, please.
B. What seems to be the problem?
A. I'm wondering (if/whether) *I broke my arm.*
B. All right. Please take a seat in the waiting room. The doctor will see you shortly.

Listening

Listen and choose where the conversation is taking place.

1. a. a clinic   b. a hospital
2. a. an office   b. a fire department
3. a. a doctor's office b. a school
4. a. an airport   b. an airplane
5. a. a book store   b. a library

Choose

1. Do you know _____?
   a. is it going to rain
   b. if it's going to rain

2. I'm not really sure _____.
   a. whether the plane will be late
   b. will the plane be late

3. The librarian can tell you _____.
   a. if the library will be open
   b. whether will the library be open

4. Can you tell me _____?
   a. where have they moved
   b. whether they have moved

5. I'm anxious to know _____.
   a. how did I do on the exam
   b. how I did on the exam

6. Jackie is wondering _____.
   a. whether she got the job
   b. did she get the job

✎ IN YOUR OWN WORDS

For Writing and Discussion

> Do you know...?
> Can you tell me...?
> Could you tell me...?
> Could you please tell me...?
> Could you possibly tell me...?
> Do you have any idea...?
> Do you by any chance know...?
> I'd like to know...
> I'm wondering...

1.

Mr. and Mrs. Grant are planning to move out of their apartment and buy a house. They're visiting a house right now and talking with a real estate agent. What questions should they ask?

They should ask how old the house is.
They should ask whether the roof leaks.
They should ask _____.

Now create a conversation between Mr. and Mrs. Grant and the real estate agent. Use some of the expressions at the top of the page in your questions.

2.

Tina is planning to buy a used car. She's visiting a used car lot right now and talking with a salesman. What questions should she ask?

She should ask whether the brakes work.
She should ask who the previous owner was.
She should ask _____.

Now create a conversation between Tina and the car salesman. Use some of the expressions at the top of the page in your questions.

3.

Michael is planning to go to college next year. He's going to apply to many different schools. He's visiting a college right now and talking with a person in the admissions office. What questions should he ask?

He should ask what courses students have to take.
He should ask if the college has a good library.
He should ask _____.

Now create a conversation between Michael and the person in the admissions office. Use some of the expressions at the top of the page in your questions.

ON YOUR OWN: I Want to Report a Missing Person!

> ### Police Department
> ### Missing Person Information Sheet
>
> 1. What is your name?
> 2. What is the missing person's name?
> 3. What is his/her address?
> 4. How old is he/she?
> 5. How tall is he/she?
> 6. How much does he/she weigh?
> 7. Does this person have any scars, birthmarks, or other special characteristics?
> 8. Where was he/she the last time you saw him/her?
> 9. What was he/she wearing at that time?
> 10. What was he/she doing?
> 11. What is your relationship to the missing person?
> 12. What is your telephone number?
> 13. When can we reach you at that number?

A student in your class is missing! Call the police!

I want to report a missing person!

1. Would you please tell me what your name is?

2. And would you tell me...

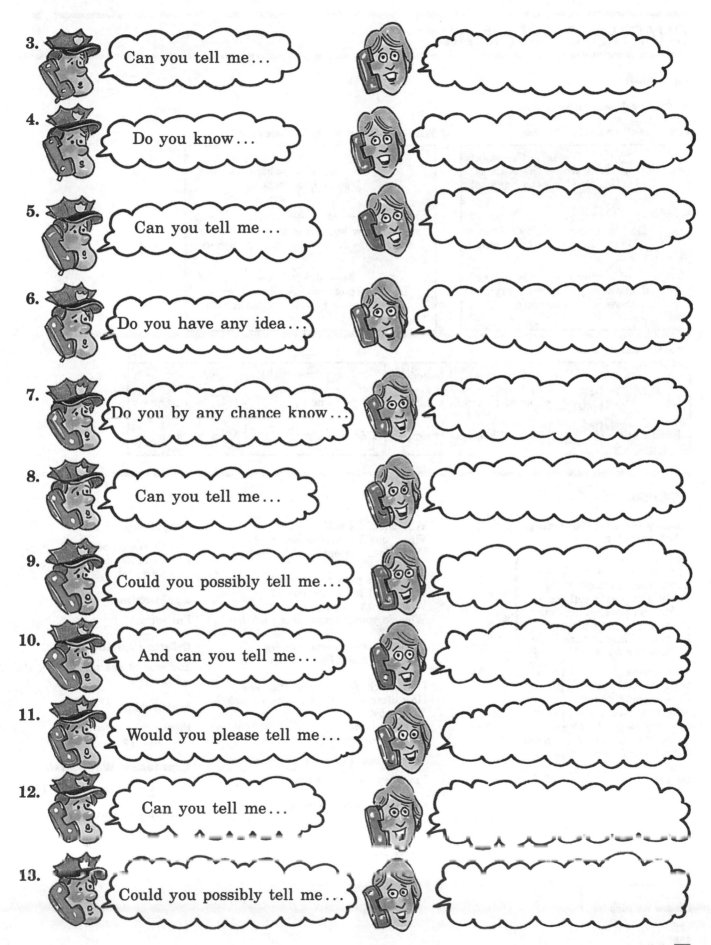

CHAPTER 3 SUMMARY

GRAMMAR

Embedded Questions:

WH-Questions with To Be

> Where is the bank?
> Do you know where the bank is?
> I don't know where the bank is.
>
> What is he doing?
> Do you know what he's doing?
> I don't know what he's doing.
>
> Why were they crying?
> Do you know why they were crying?
> I don't know why they were crying.

Wh-Questions with Do/Does/Did

> Where does he live?
> Do you know where he lives?
> I don't know where he lives.
>
> How often do they come here?
> Do you know how often they come here?
> I don't know how often they come here.
>
> How did she break her leg?
> Do you know how she broke her leg?
> I don't know how she broke her leg.

Yes/No Questions

> Is Tom in school today?
> Do you know {if / whether} Tom is in school today?
> I don't know {if / whether} Tom is in school today.

> Does Mary work here?
> Do you know {if / whether} Mary works here?
> I don't know {if / whether} Mary works here.

FUNCTIONS

Asking for and Reporting Information

Do you know
Can you tell me
Could you tell me
Could you please tell me
Could you possibly tell me
Do you have any idea
Do you by any chance know
} *where the bank is?*

Who knows
Who can tell me
Does anyone know
Who remembers
Can anybody tell me
} *who the nineteenth president of the United States was?*

Do you know {if / whether} *Tom is in school today?*

I'm wondering {if / whether} *I broke my arm.*

I don't know
I don't remember
I can't remember
I've forgotten
I'm not sure
I have no idea
} *where the money is.*

Who *should I call?*
What *was his license number?*
What does *the bank robber* look like?
What time does *the movie* begin?
When will *the train* arrive?
Where *is the money?*
Why *do young people like such loud music?*
How *did Doris break her leg?*
How long *has Alan been working here?*
How much *do eggs* cost *this week?*
How often *does the ice cream truck come by?*
How old is *he?*
Whose *dog* is this?

What seems to be the problem?

I'm sorry. I don't know.

Expressing Uncertainty

I don't know
I'm not sure
I have no idea
} *where the money is.*

Forgetting

I don't remember
I can't remember
I've forgotten
} *where the money is.*

Apologizing

I'm sorry.

Offering Advice

You should *ask the man at the box office.*

Instructing

Please *take a seat in the waiting room.*

Expressing Want-Desire

I'd like to *see the doctor,* please.

Complimenting

Very good, *class!*

Perfect Modals:
Should Have ▪
Must Have ▪
Might Have ▪
May Have ▪
Could Have ▪

He Should Have Spoken Louder

I	
He	
She	
It	should have eaten.
We	
You	
They	

A. Did Richard speak loud enough in the school play last night?

B. No, he didn't. He **should have spoken** louder.

1. Did Bob drive carefully enough during his driving test?
   more carefully

2. Did Lucy study hard enough for the Social Studies quiz?
   harder

3. Did Theodore practice long enough for his piano lesson?
   longer

4. Did Mr. and Mrs. Gleason get to the airport early enough?
   earlier

5. Did Andrew write legibly enough on his English exam?
   more legibly

6. Did Harriet take her chocolate cake out of the oven soon enough?
   sooner

7. Did Sally speak confidently enough at her job interview?
   more confidently

8. Did Mr. Johnson dress comfortably enough for his first yoga class?
   more comfortably

THEY DIDN'T DO AS WELL AS THEY SHOULD HAVE

Gloria didn't do as well as she should have at a job interview today. She didn't get the job, and she realizes now that she should have done a few things differently. She should have spoken more confidently, she should have told more about her previous experience, and she probably should have worn more conservative clothes.

In addition, she shouldn't have arrived late for the interview. She shouldn't have smoked in the interviewer's office. And she DEFINITELY shouldn't have asked so many questions about vacations and sick days. Gloria will certainly do things differently the next time she has a job interview!

Arthur didn't do as well as he should have at a tennis tournament yesterday. He didn't win, and he realizes now that he should have done a few things differently. He should have practiced more during the week, he should have done more warm-up exercises before the tournament, and he probably should have gotten a good night's sleep the night before.

Furthermore, he shouldn't have used his old tennis racket. He shouldn't have eaten such a large breakfast that morning. And he DEFINITELY shouldn't have gone out dancing with his friends the night before. Arthur will certainly do a few things differently the next time he plays in a tennis tournament!

CHECK-UP

True, False, or Maybe?

Answer True, False, or Maybe (if the answer isn't in the story).

1. Gloria didn't speak confidently about herself at the interview.
2. She didn't get the job because she didn't have previous experience.
3. Gloria likes to go on vacations and gets sick very often.
4. Arthur didn't practice for the tennis tournament.
5. He used his old tennis racket during the tournament.
6. Arthur's friends think that going dancing is more fun than playing tennis.

Listening

Listen and choose the best answer based on the conversation you hear.

1. a. He should have spoken softer.
   b. He should have spoken louder.

2. a. They should have gotten there earlier.
   b. They should have left later.

3. a. He should have dressed more comfortably.
   b. He should have spoken more confidently.

4. a. He should have left them in the oven longer.
   b. He should have taken them out of the oven sooner.

5. a. She should have gotten a good night's sleep last night.
   b. She should have gotten up earlier this morning.

6. a. He should have written more legibly.
   b. He should have studied harder.

What's Your Opinion?

1. What should Gloria do the next time she has a job interview?
2. What should Arthur do the next time he plays in a tennis tournament?

Tell about a time when you didn't do as well as you should have. What was the situation? What should you have done differently?

IN YOUR OWN WORDS

For Writing and Discussion

*"You should" = "a person should."

What should you do if you want to do well at a job interview?

What should you talk about?
What should you ask about?
What should you wear?
What should you bring with you?
When should you arrive?

(In your answers, use "You should.")*

He Must Have Overslept

I
He
She
It } must have eaten.
We
You
They

A. Mr. Jones came to work late today.

B. I'm really surprised to hear that. He NEVER comes to work late!

A. I know. He **must have overslept**.

1. Sherman went to the doctor yesterday.
   feel very bad

2. Beverly yelled at me today.
   be upset

3. Peter made a lot of mistakes in his homework.
   have trouble with the lesson

4. Mr. Crabapple smiled at his employees this morning.
   be in a very good mood

5. Judy refused to eat her dinner last night.
   eat too many cookies after school

6. Maria missed English class all last week.
   be very sick

7. You talked in your sleep last night.
   have a bad dream

8. Walter was in a terrible mood today.
   "get up on the wrong side of the bed"

49

I'm a Little Concerned

$$\left.\begin{array}{l} \text{I} \\ \text{He} \\ \text{She} \\ \text{It} \\ \text{We} \\ \text{You} \\ \text{They} \end{array}\right\} \text{might/may have eaten.}$$

A. John looks tired! He **must have swum fifty laps** today.

B. I'm not so sure. He $\left\{\begin{array}{l} \textbf{MIGHT} \\ \textbf{MAY} \end{array}\right\}$ **have swum fifty laps**, but that doesn't usually make him so tired.

A. I'm a little concerned. Maybe we should talk with him.

B. That's a good idea.

A. Barbara looks upset! She **must have failed an exam** today.

B. I'm not so sure. She $\left\{\begin{array}{l} \textbf{MIGHT} \\ \textbf{MAY} \end{array}\right\}$ **have failed an exam**, but that doesn't usually make her so upset.

A. I'm a little concerned. Maybe we should talk with her.

B. That's a good idea.

1. Fred looks tired!
work overtime

2. Peggy looks exhausted!
jog a little too much

3. Wayne looks upset!
have an argument with the boss

4. Senator Johnson looks tired!
shake* a lot of hands

5. Roger looks upset!
have a fight with his girlfriend

6. Our English teacher looks angry!
find a lot of mistakes in our homework

7. Martha looks jittery!
drink† too much coffee

8. Our cat looks scared!
be chased by the dog across the street

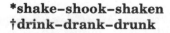

*shake–shook–shaken
†drink–drank–drunk

He Could Have Broken His Back!

I
He
She
It
We
You
They
} could have eaten.

A. You won't believe what George did yesterday!

B. What did he do?

A. He moved his piano by himself!

B. You're kidding! He shouldn't have done that!

A. Of course he shouldn't have! He {**could** / **might**} have broken his back!

1. *go hiking by himself in the mountains*
   get lost

2. *eat all the ice cream in the refrigerator*
   get sick

3. go skating on the town pond
   fall* through the ice

4. play baseball in the rain
   catch a bad cold

5. ride her bicycle downtown during
      rush hour
   get hurt

6. swim to the other side of the lake
   drown

7. try to fix their TV by themselves
   be electrocuted

8. shout at the boss
   get fired

9. run in the Boston Marathon
   have a heart attack

10. mix nitric acid and glycerin
    blow† up the school

11. get into an argument with
       a policeman
    wind up in jail

12.

*fall–fell–fallen
†blow–blew–blown

I Owe You an Apology

A. You know, I owe you an apology.

B. What for?

A. You must have been very angry with me yesterday.

B. I don't understand. Why should I have been angry with you?

A. Don't you remember? We had planned to **see a movie** yesterday, but I completely forgot!

B. Don't worry about it. Actually, I owe YOU an apology.

A. You do? Why?

B. I couldn't have **seen a movie** with you anyway. I had to **take care of my little sister** yesterday . . . and I completely forgot to tell you.

A. That's okay. Maybe we can **see a movie** some time soon.

A. You know, I owe you an apology.

B. What for?

A. You must have been very angry with me yesterday.

B. I don't understand. Why should I have been angry with you?

A. Don't you remember? We had planned to _____ yesterday, but I completely forgot!

B. Don't worry about it. Actually, I owe YOU an apology.

A. You do? Why?

B. I couldn't have _____ with you anyway. I had to _____ yesterday . . . and I completely forgot to tell you.

A. That's okay. Maybe we can _____ some time soon.

1. *go to the mall*
   go to the doctor

2. *have lunch*
   go to an important meeting

3. *work out at the fitness club*
   visit a friend in the hospital

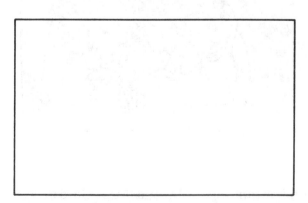

4.

LUCKY PEOPLE

Gary must have been daydreaming while he was driving to work yesterday. He drove through a red light at the busiest intersection in town. Fortunately, he didn't hit anybody. Gary was pretty lucky. He could have caused a terrible accident.

Mrs. Chen must have been very scared yesterday. There was a big, mean dog outside while she was putting out the garbage. Fortunately, the dog was chained to a fence. Mrs. Chen was pretty lucky. She might have been bitten.

Howard must have been extremely irritable yesterday. He got into a big argument with his supervisor over something very unimportant. Fortunately, his supervisor didn't get angry. Howard was very lucky. He could have gotten fired.

Mrs. Wilson must have been feeling very brave this morning. She refused to hand over her purse to a man who was trying to mug her. Fortunately, he got scared and ran away. Mrs. Wilson was very lucky. She might have gotten hurt . . . or even killed!

Mr. and Mrs. Carson must have been having a lot of financial problems last year. They were never able to pay their rent on time. Fortunately, their landlord was very understanding. Mr. and Mrs. Carson were pretty lucky. They could have been evicted.

Irwin must have been very lonely last night. He spent the entire evening making long distance phone calls to his friends all over the country. Fortunately, most of his friends weren't home. Irwin was pretty lucky. He could have run up quite a big phone bill this month.

1. Tell about a time when something bad *could have* happened to you, but *didn't*. What was the situation? What could have happened?

2. Tell about a time when you were . . . . lonely.
. . . . scared.
. . . . irritable.
. . . . brave.

READING

Natasha George Henry Mr. and Mrs. Ramirez
Nicole Mr. and Mrs. Sato Maria

GEORGE DIDN'T COME TO ENGLISH CLASS

George didn't come to his English class yesterday evening, and all the students in the class are wondering why.

Natasha thinks he might have gotten sick. Henry thinks he might have had a doctor's appointment. Mr. and Mrs. Ramirez think that one of George's children may have been sick. Nicole thinks he may have had to work overtime. Mr. and Mrs. Sato think he might have gone to the airport to meet his relatives who are arriving from overseas. And Maria thinks he may have decided to study in another school.

All the students are curious about why George didn't come to English class yesterday evening . . . and they're a little concerned.

IN YOUR OWN WORDS

For Writing and Discussion

Tell a story using this model as a guide.

Our English teacher didn't come to class today, and all the students are wondering why.

_____ thinks _____.
_____ thinks _____.
.
.

And I think _____.

We're all curious about why our English teacher didn't come to class today . . . and we're a little concerned.

CHAPTER 4 *SUMMARY*

GRAMMAR

Perfect Modals:

Should Have

I He She It We You They	should have eaten.

Must Have

I He She It We You They	must have been upset.

Might Have/May Have

I He She It We You They	might have may have	eaten.

Could Have

I He She It We You They	could have gotten lost.

FUNCTIONS

Expressing Possibility

He might have *swum fifty laps.*
He may have *swum fifty laps.*

He could have *broken his back!*
He might have *broken his back!*

Making a Deduction

He must have *overslept.*

Expressing an Opinion

He should have *spoken louder.*

He shouldn't have *done that!*

Expressing Agreement

I know.

That's a good idea.

Of course *he shouldn't have.*

Expressing Disagreement

I'm not so sure.

Describing Feelings-Emotions

I'm a little concerned.

Tell about a time when you were lonely/scared/irritable/brave.

Offering a Suggestion

Maybe we should *talk with him.*

Initiating a Topic

You won't believe *what George did yesterday!*

You know, . . .

Expressing Surprise-Disbelief

I'm really surprised to hear that.

You're kidding!

Asking for and Reporting Information

Did *Richard speak loud* enough *in the school play last night?*

What did *he* do?

Why *should I have been angry at you?*

Inquiring about Remembering

Don't you remember?

Forgetting

I completely forgot!
I completely forgot to *tell you.*

Expressing Inability

I couldn't have *seen a movie with you.*

Expressing Obligation

I had to *take care of my little sister yesterday.*

Apologizing

I owe you an apology.

Responding to an Apology

Don't worry about it.

Indicating Lack of Understanding

I don't understand.

Focusing Attention

Actually, . . .

Conditional:
Present Real
(If_____Will) ■
Present Unreal
(If_____Would) ■
Hope Clauses ■

They Aren't Sure

if _____ will _____

A. What are you going to do this weekend?

B. We aren't sure.
If the weather is good, we'll probably go to the beach.
If the weather is bad, we'll probably stay home.

1. How is Tom going to get to work tomorrow?

He isn't sure.
If it rains, _____.
If it's sunny, _____.

2. What are Mr. and Mrs. Green going to do tonight?

They aren't sure.
If they're tired, _____.
If they have some energy, _____.

3. Where are you going to have lunch today?

I'm not sure.
If I'm in a hurry, _____.
If I have some time, _____.

4. What's Jane going to do tomorrow?

She isn't sure.
If she still has a cold, _____.
If she feels better, _____.

5. Where is Patty going to go after school today?

She isn't sure.
If she has a lot of homework, _____.
If she doesn't have a lot of homework,
_____.

6. What's Henry going to have for dessert this evening?

He isn't sure.
If he decides to stay on his diet, ___.
If he decides to forget about his diet,
_____.

Do You Think...?

A. Do you think Johnny should go to school today?

B. No, I don't. If Johnny goes to school today, he might **give his cold to the other children.**

1. Do you think I should put some more salt in this soup?

   spoil it

2. Do you think I should skip English class today?

   miss something important

3. Do you think Rover should come to the beach with us?

   get carsick

4. Do you think I should try to break up that fight?

   get hurt

5. Do you think Mary should quit her job?

   have trouble finding another one

6. Do you think Teddy should stay up and watch TV with us?

   have trouble getting up in the morning

7. Do you think I should marry Norman?

   regret it for the rest of your life

8.

I Hope

I hope it rains tomorrow.
I hope it doesn't rain tomorrow.

A. Do you think it'll be a hot summer?

B. I hope not. If **it's a hot summer**, our classroom will be very warm. And if **our classroom is very warm**, it'll be impossible to study English!

A. You're right. I hope **it isn't a hot summer.**

1.

A. Do you think the train will be crowded?

B. I hope not.
If _____, we'll have to stand. And if _____, we'll be exhausted by the time we get to work!

A. You're right. I hope _____.

2.

A. Do you think the boss will retire this year?

B. I hope not.
If _____, his son will take his place.
And if _____, everybody will quit!

A. You're right. I hope _____.

3.

A. Do you think it'll be very cold tonight?

B. I hope not.
If _____, our car won't start in the morning.
And if _____, we'll have to walk to work!

A. You're right. I hope _____.

4.

A. Do you think our math teacher will give us a quiz tomorrow?

B. I hope not.
If _____, we'll do poorly on it.
And if _____, our parents will be very upset!

A. You're right. I hope _____.

5.

A. Do you think it'll rain tomorrow?

B. I hope not.
If _____, we'll have to cancel the school picnic.
And if _____, everybody will be very disappointed!

A. You're right. I hope _____.

6.

A. Do you think the bus will be late today?

B. I hope not.
If _____, we won't get to work on time.
And if _____, the boss will be very angry!

A. You're right. I hope _____.

7.

A. Do you think inflation will get worse this year?

B. I hope not.
If _____, I'll have to get a second job.
And if _____, my family will be very upset!

A. You're right. I hope _____.

8.

A. Do you think our landlord will raise the rent this year?

B. I hope not.
If _____, we won't be able to pay it.
And if _____, we'll have to move!

A. You're right. I hope _____.

9.

A. Do you think our TV will be at the repair shop for a long time?

B. I hope not.
If _____, we won't have anything to do in the evening.
And if _____, we'll go crazy!

A. You're right. I hope _____.

THE WISHING WELL

There's a park in the center of Danville, and in the park there's a wishing well. This wishing well is a very popular spot with the people of Danville. Every day people pass by the wishing well, drop in a coin, and make a wish. Some people make wishes about their jobs, others make wishes about the weather, and lots of people make wishes about their families and friends.

Today is a particularly busy day at the wishing well. Many people are coming by and making wishes about their hopes for the future.

Ralph hopes he sells a lot of used cars this month. If he sells a lot of used cars, he'll receive a large Christmas bonus.

Patricia hopes she gets a raise soon. If she gets a raise, her family will be able to take a vacation.

Nancy and Paul hope they find a cheap apartment soon. If they find a cheap apartment, they won't have to live with Paul's parents anymore.

Andy hopes it snows tomorrow. If it snows tomorrow, his school might be closed.

Lana hopes her next movie is a big success. If it's a big success, she'll be rich and famous.

John hopes he gets good grades on his next report card. If he gets good grades, his parents will buy him the radio he has wanted for a long time.

Mr. and Mrs. Clark hope they live to be a hundred. If they live to be a hundred, they'll be able to watch their grandchildren and great-grandchildren grow up.

J.P. Morgan hopes the nation's economy improves next year. If the economy improves next year, his company's profits will increase.

And Wendy hopes she gets accepted into medical school. If she gets accepted into medical school, she'll become a doctor, just like her father and grandfather.

You can see why the wishing well is a very popular spot with the people of Danville. Day after day, people pass by, drop in their coins, and hope that their wishes come true.

✔ CHECK-UP

Q & A

You're talking with the people in the story above. Using this model, create dialogs based on the story.

A. I hope *I sell a lot of used cars this month.*
B. Oh?
A. Yes. If *I sell a lot of used cars, I'll receive a large Christmas bonus.*
B. Oh, really? Well, good luck! I hope *you sell a lot of used cars!*
A. Thanks.

Choose

1. We hope our landlord doesn't ____ our rent.
   a. improve
   b. increase

2. Have you ____ today's mail yet?
   a. received
   b. accepted

3. Jennifer is very smart. She gets good ____ in all her subjects.
   a. grades
   b. cards

4. The company couldn't increase my salary this year, but they gave me a very nice ____.
   a. raise
   b. bonus

5. Arthur hopes his new Broadway play is a big ____.
   a. profit
   b. success

6. The President is very proud of the country's ____.
   a. inflation
   b. economy

If They Had More Time, They'd Visit Us More Often

(I would)	I'd
(He would)	He'd
(She would)	She'd
(It would)	It'd
(We would)	We'd
(You would)	You'd
(They would)	They'd

} work.

if _____ would _____

A. Why don't our grandchildren visit us more often?

B. They don't have enough time.
If they had more time, they'd visit us more often.

A. Why isn't Melvin a good salesman?

B. He isn't aggressive enough.
If he were* more aggressive, he'd be a good salesman.

*If [I, he, she, it, we, you, they] were...

1. A. Why doesn't Sally get good grades?

B. She doesn't study enough.
If _____.

2. A. Why isn't Mark a good driver?

B. He isn't careful enough.
If _____.

3. **A.** Why don't I feel energetic?
   B. You don't sleep enough.
      If _____.

4. **A.** Why doesn't Alexander enjoy playing baseball?
   B. He isn't athletic enough.
      If _____.

5. **A.** Why doesn't Julie have friends at school?
   B. She isn't outgoing enough.
      If _____.

6. **A.** Why doesn't Sidney have a yearly checkup?
   B. He isn't concerned enough about his health.
      If _____.

7. **A.** Why aren't you satisfied with your jobs?
   B. We don't get paid enough.
      If _____.

8. **A.** Why don't I enjoy life?
   B. You aren't relaxed enough.
      If _____.

9. **A.** Why aren't most Americans in good physical condition?
   B. They don't exercise enough.
      If _____.

10. **A.** Why don't Tom and Janet get along with each other?
    B. They don't have enough in common.
       If _____.

11. **A.** Why don't our congressmen do something about pollution?
    B. They aren't concerned enough about the environment.
       If _____.

12. **A.** Why doesn't our English teacher buy a new pair of shoes?
    B. He doesn't make enough money.
       If _____.

If He Didn't Like His Job, He Wouldn't Work So Hard

if _____ wouldn't (would not) _____

A. I wonder why Fred works so hard.

B. I don't know. He must like his job.

A. You're probably right.
If he didn't like his job, he wouldn't work so hard.

A. I wonder why my older brother and his girlfriend hold hands all the time.

B. I don't know. They must be in love.

A. You're probably right.
If they weren't in love, they wouldn't hold hands all the time.

1. I wonder why Barbara wants to be a schoolteacher.
   She must like children.

2. I wonder why Alan makes so many mistakes.
   He must be careless.

3. I wonder why Nancy is so nervous.
She must have an exam today.

4. I wonder why our teacher is shouting at us today.
She must be in a bad mood.

5. I wonder why Rover is barking at the door.
He must want to go outside.

6. I wonder why Bob is so dressed up today.
He must be going to a job interview.

7. I wonder why John gets into so many fights.
He must like to argue with people.

8. I wonder why Judy wants a telescope for her birthday.
She must be interested in astronomy.

9. I wonder why Jeff is home tonight.
He must have to take care of his little brother.

10. I wonder why Shirley goes hiking in the mountains every weekend.
She must enjoy being outdoors.

11. I wonder why I'm sneezing so much.
You must be allergic to my perfume.

12.

THEY WOULD BE WILLING TO IF...

For several months, Mrs. Hopkins has been pressuring her husband, Albert, to go to the dentist, but he refuses to go. The reason is that he can't stand the sound of the dentist's drill. Albert says that if the dentist's drill didn't bother him so much, he would be willing to go to the dentist. Mrs. Hopkins hopes her husband changes his mind and goes to the dentist soon.

For several months, Barbara's family has been encouraging her to ask her boss for a raise, but Barbara refuses to do it. The reason is that she's afraid he might get angry and say "No." Barbara says that if she weren't afraid of her boss's reaction, she would be willing to ask for a raise. Barbara's family hopes she changes her mind and asks for a raise soon.

For several months, Senator Johnson's assistants have been urging him to run for the presidency, but he refuses to do it. The reason is that he doesn't have enough money to pay for all the television commercials and other campaign expenses. Senator Johnson says that if he had sufficient funds, he would be willing to run. Senator Johnson's assistants hope he changes his mind and runs for the presidency soon.

✔ CHECK-UP

Listening

Listen and choose the statement that is true based on what you hear.

1. a. Albert wasn't afraid of the dentist's drill.
   b. Albert is afraid of the dentist's drill.

2. a. Senator Johnson has enough money.
   b. Senator Johnson isn't interested in running for the presidency.

3. a. Mrs. Jones isn't her math teacher.
   b. Mrs. Jones is her math teacher.

4. a. They might receive bonuses.
   b. The company's profits didn't increase.

5. a. He isn't allergic to trees.
   b. He isn't going hiking this weekend.

6. a. He isn't going to the movies tonight.
   b. He doesn't have to work tonight.

Answer these questions and ask other students.

1. What would you do if you saw someone choking on a piece of food?

2. What would you do if you saw someone having a heart attack?

3. What would you do if you were at the beach and you saw someone drowning?

4. What would you do if somebody in your family were missing?

5. What would you do if somebody came up to you on the street and tried to rob you?

6. What would you do if a fire broke out in your house or apartment?

7. What would you do if you were lying in bed and you heard someone trying to break into your house or apartment?

8. What would you do if you were bitten by a dog?

Think of some other emergencies and ask other students if they're prepared:

GRAMMAR

Present Real Conditional (if—will)

If	I we you they	feel	better,	I'll we'll you'll they'll	eat dinner.
	he she it	feels		he'll she'll it'll	

Present Unreal Conditional (if—would)

If	I he she we you they	had more time,	I'd he'd she'd we'd you'd they'd	study more often.

If	I he she we you they	didn't have an exam today,	I he she we you they	**wouldn't** be nervous.

Hope-Clauses

I We You They	hope	I we you they	get	a raise soon.
He She	hopes	he she	gets	

I hope it rains tomorrow.
I hope it doesn't rain tomorrow.

I hope it's warm tonight.
I hope it isn't cold tonight.

FUNCTIONS

Inquiring about Intention

What are you going to do *this weekend*?

What would you do if *you saw someone choking on a piece of food*?

Expressing Probability

If *the weather is good, we'll* probably *go to the beach.*

If *Johnny goes to school today, he* might *give his cold to the other children.*

If *it's a hot summer, our classroom* will *be very warm.*

Expressing Uncertainty

We aren't sure.

Inquiring about Probability

Do you think it'll be *a hot summer?*

Inquiring about an Opinion

Do you think *Johnny should go to school today?*

Asking for and Reporting Information

I wonder why *Fred works so hard.*

I don't know.

Expressing Hope

I hope not.

I hope *it isn't a hot summer.*

Expressing Agreement

You're right.
You're probably right.

Making a Deduction

He must *like his job.*

Responding to Information

Oh?

Oh, really?

Present Unreal Conditional (continued) ■
Wish-Clauses ■

If I Were You

A. Do you think the boss would be angry if I went home early?

B. Yes, I do. As a matter of fact, I think she'd be VERY angry.

A. Do you really think so?

B. Yes. I'm positive. I wouldn't go home early if I were you.

A. I suppose you're right.

1. Do you think Roger would be disappointed if I missed his birthday party?

2. Do you think our English teacher would be upset if I skipped class tomorrow?

3. Do you think Mom and Dad would be angry if I borrowed the car?

4. Do you think our neighbors would be annoyed if I turned on the stereo?

5. Do you think Jack would be jealous if I took out his girlfriend?

6. Do you think the voters would be upset if I raised taxes?

7. Do you think Jennifer would be mad if I rode her bicycle?

8. Do you think the landlord would be upset if I painted the kitchen purple?

9. Do you think my parents would be disappointed if I dropped out of school?

10. Do you think my fans would be unhappy if I got a haircut?

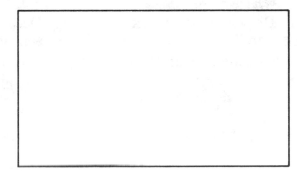

11. Do you think Tom would be embarrassed if I showed his girlfriend a photograph of him in the bathtub when he was two years old?

12.

Wishes

| Tom **lives** in Boston. | He **wishes** he **lived** in New York. |

A. Do you enjoy driving a school bus?

B. Not really. I wish I drove a taxi.

A. Does Mr. Robinson enjoy being a teacher?

B. Not really. He wishes he were an actor.

1. Does Mary enjoy living in the suburbs?

in the city

2. Does Mrs. Kramer enjoy teaching math?

something else

3. Does Larry enjoy being single?

married

4. Do you enjoy working here?

someplace else

5. Does Ralph enjoy selling used cars?

insurance

6. Does Oscar enjoy painting houses?

portraits

7. Do you enjoy being the vice-president?

the president

8. Does Sarah enjoy having two part-time jobs?

one good full-time job

9.

SICK AND TIRED

Frank is "sick and tired" of selling insurance! He has been doing that for twenty-eight years. Frank wishes he sold something else. In fact, at this point in his life, he would be willing to sell ANYTHING, as long as it wasn't insurance!

Mrs. Watson is "sick and tired" of teaching seventh-grade math! She has been teaching that subject for the past eighteen years. Mrs. Watson wishes she taught something else. In fact, at this point in her life, she would be willing to teach ANYTHING, as long as it wasn't seventh-grade math!

Jerry is "sick and tired" of writing want ads and obituaries for the *Midville Times*! He has been doing that since 1959. Jerry wishes he wrote something else. In fact, at this point in his life, he'd be willing to write ANYTHING, as long as it wasn't want ads and obituaries!

Susie and her brother are "sick and tired" of eating peanut butter and jelly sandwiches for lunch every day. They have been eating that for lunch every day for the past four years. Susie and her brother wish their mother would give them something else for lunch. In fact, at this point in their lives, they would be willing to eat ANYTHING for lunch, as long as it wasn't peanut butter and jelly sandwiches!

 *CHECK-UP*

Choose

1. Bob found his job through the _____.
   a. want ads
   b. obituaries

2. I was very _____ when my supervisor shouted at me in front of all the other employees.
   a. jealous
   b. embarrassed

3. Henry _____ the meeting because he had to go to the dentist.
   a. dropped out of
   b. skipped

4. After our house was robbed, I realized how important it is to have _____.
   a. insurance
   b. taxes

5. If you don't visit Aunt Nellie in the hospital, she'll be very _____.
   a. sick and tired
   b. disappointed

6. This is a _____ of me that was painted when I was three years old.
   a. photography
   b. portrait

They Wish They Could

A. Can Jonathan dance?

B. No, he can't . . . but he wishes he could.
If he could dance, he'd **go dancing every night**.

1. Can Mary sew?
make all her own clothes

2. Can Steve use a computer?
be able to get a better job

3. Can Gloria find her keys?
be able to get into her apartment

4. Can Richard find his glasses?
watch TV tonight

5. Can Janet type fast?
be able to leave work on time

6. Can Henry fix his car by himself?
save a lot of money

7. Can Maria stop thinking about tomorrow's English test?
get a good night's sleep

8. Can Ronald play a musical instrument?
be able to march in the school parade

9. Can Jessica talk?
tell her parents she doesn't like her baby food

10.

Why Do You Say That?

if _____ {could / would be able to} _____

My landlord is going to repaint my apartment this Saturday.

A. You know, I wish my landlord weren't going to repaint my apartment this Saturday.

B. Oh? Why do you say that?

A. If my landlord weren't going to repaint my apartment, {I could / I'd be able to} go away for the weekend.

B. Oh. I see.

My son wants to be a dentist.

A. You know, I wish my son didn't want to be a dentist.

B. Oh? Why do you say that?

A. If my son didn't want to be a dentist, {I could / I'd be able to} train him to manage my shoe store when I retire.

B. Oh. I see.

1. The weather is going to be nice this weekend.

   wear my new raincoat for the first time

2. The boss wants to take me to dinner tomorrow.

   go home early

3. The TV is fixed.

   talk to the children

4. My daughter is going to a college out of town.

   see her more often

5. I live in a high-rise building.

   have a garden

6. My son takes drum lessons.

   have some "peace and quiet" around the house

7. My new office has a view of the park.

   concentrate more on my work

8. We're studying difficult grammar now.

   do my homework in just a few minutes

READING

Mr. Anderson   Mrs. Anderson

Michael   Jennifer   Steven

THEY WISH THEY LIVED IN THE CITY

The Anderson family lives in the suburbs, but they wish they lived in the city. If they lived in the city, Mr. Anderson wouldn't have to spend all his spare time mowing the lawn and working around the house. Mrs. Anderson wouldn't have to spend two hours commuting to work every day. Their son Michael would be able to take the bus to the baseball stadium. Their daughter, Jennifer, would be living close to all of her favorite book stores. And their other son, Steven, could visit the zoo more often. It would be very difficult for the Anderson family to move to the city now, but perhaps some day they'll be able to. They certainly hope so.

✔CHECK-UP

Listening

Listen and write the missing words.

Mrs. Burton   Mr. Burton

Ken   Betsy and Kathy   Tiger

THEY WISH THEY LIVED IN THE SUBURBS

The Burton family lives in the city, but they _____ they lived in the suburbs. If they _____ in the suburbs, Mrs. Burton _____ be able to plant a garden and grow vegetables. Mr. Burton _____ have to listen to the noisy city traffic all the time. Their son, Ken, _____ a backyard to play in. Their daughters, Betsy and Kathy, _____ share a room. And their cat, Tiger, _____ go outside and roam around and play with the other cats. It _____ very difficult for the Burton family to move to the suburbs now, but perhaps some day _____. They certainly hope so.

How about YOU?

1. Do you wish you lived someplace else? Where? Why?
2. Compare life in the city and life in the suburbs. What are the advantages and disadvantages of each?

81

Do You Want My Honest Opinion?

A. Would you mind if I asked you for some advice?

B. No, not at all.

A. I'm thinking of **buying a used car from Ralph Jones**, but I'm not sure that's a very good idea. What do you think?

B. Do you want my honest opinion?

A. Yes, of course.

B. Well . . . to tell the truth, I wouldn't **buy a used car from Ralph Jones** if I were you.

A. Oh?

B. Yes. If you **bought a used car from Ralph Jones**, you'd probably **spend a lot of money on repairs**.

A. Hmm. You might be right. Thanks for the advice.

1. *ask the boss for a raise this week*
   get fired

2. *grow a moustache*
   look very funny

3. *work overtime this weekend*
   be exhausted by Monday morning

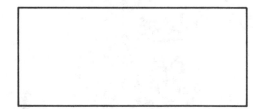

4.

ALL THUMBS

Ethel can never fix anything around the house. In fact, everybody tells her she's "all thumbs." She wishes she were more mechanically inclined. If she were more mechanically inclined, she would be able to repair things around the house by herself.

Robert can't dance very well. In fact, all the girls he goes out with tell him he has "two left feet." Robert wishes he could dance better. If he could dance better, he wouldn't feel so self-conscious when he goes out dancing.

Maria is having a hard time learning English. She's having a lot of trouble with English grammar and pronunciation. Maria wishes she had a "better ear" for languages. If she had a "better ear" for languages, she probably wouldn't be having so much trouble in her English class.

✔ CHECK-UP

Match

Try to match the following expressions with the descriptions on the right.

_____ 1. He's *handy* around the house.
_____ 2. She has a green *thumb*.
_____ 3. He's very *nosey*.
_____ 4. She shoots from the *hip*.
_____ 5. He's all *heart*.
_____ 6. They've got a lot on their *shoulders*.
_____ 7. He's up in *arms*.
_____ 8. She always keeps her *chin* up.

a. very angry
b. very honest and blunt
c. optimistic
d. knows how to fix things
e. has many responsibilities
f. good at gardening
g. very kind
h. asks about other people

How about YOU?

Are you "all thumbs"? Do you have "two left feet"? Everybody has a few things he or she would like to do better. What do you wish you could do better? Why?

CHAPTER 6 *SUMMARY*

GRAMMAR

Present Unreal Conditional (If—would)

Do you think the boss **would** be angry **if** I went home early?
I **wouldn't** go home early **if** I were you.

If	I he she we you they	could use a computer,	I'd he'd she'd we'd you'd they'd	be able to get a better job.

If the TV weren't fixed,	I could I'd be able to	talk to the children.

Wish-Clauses

I We You They	wish	I we you they	lived in New York. were more athletic. could dance. didn't live in a big building. weren't going to have a birthday party.
He She	wishes	he she	

FUNCTIONS

Asking for Advice

Would you mind if I asked you for some advice?

I'm thinking of *buying a used car*, but I'm not sure that's a very good idea. What do you think?

Offering Advice

I wouldn't *go home early* if I were you.

Do you want my honest opinion?

Responding to Advice

I suppose you're right.

You might be right.

Thanks for the advice.

Expressing Probability

If *you bought a used car from Ralph Jones, you'd* probably spend a lot of money on repairs.

Inquiring about an Opinion

Do you think *the boss would be angry if I went home early*?

Do you really think so?

Expressing an Opinion

I think *she'd be very angry*.

Wishing

I wish *I drove a taxi*.
He wishes *he were an actor*.

I wish *my landlord* weren't *going to repaint my apartment this Saturday*.

Inquiring about Satisfaction

Do you enjoy *driving a school bus*?

Inquiring about Ability

Can *Jonathan dance*?

Expressing Certainty

I'm positive.

Asking for and Reporting Information

Why do you say that?

Responding to Information

Oh?

Indicating Understanding

Oh. I see.

Hesitating

Well, . . .

Hmm.

Initiating a Topic

You know, . . .

Focusing Attention

As a matter of fact, . . .

Past Unreal Conditional
(If _____ Would Have) ■
Wish-Clauses (continued) ■

If He Had Known...

| if _____ would have _____ | I He She It We You They } would have eaten. |

A. Why didn't Peter take his umbrella to work today?

B. He didn't know it was going to rain.
If he had known it was going to rain, he would have taken his umbrella to work.

A. Why weren't you in class yesterday?

B. I wasn't feeling well.
If I had been feeling well, I would have been in class.

1. **A.** Why didn't you do your homework last night?

   B. I didn't bring my book home.
   If _____.

2. **A.** Why wasn't Sally on time for work this morning?

   B. Her alarm clock didn't ring.
   If _____.

3. **A.** Why didn't you send me a postcard?

   B. We didn't remember your address.
   If _____.

5. **A.** Why didn't you come* to the party last night?

   B. I wasn't invited.
   If _____.

7. **A.** Why didn't you make your beds this morning?

   B. We didn't have enough time.
   If _____.

9. **A.** Why didn't Mr. and Mrs. Green enjoy the play last night?

   B. They didn't have good seats.
   If _____.

11. **A.** Why didn't Harry stop at that traffic light?

    B. He wasn't looking.
    If _____.

4. **A.** Why didn't Mr. and Mrs. Clark watch the President's speech last night?

   B. Their TV wasn't working.
   If _____.

6. **A.** Why didn't Mrs. Brown's students give her a birthday present?

   B. She didn't tell them it was her birthday.
   If _____.

8. **A.** Why didn't you go to the movies with your friends last night?

   B. I wasn't in the mood to see a film.
   If _____.

10. **A.** Why wasn't Senator Maxwell re-elected?

    B. The people didn't trust him.
    If _____.

12. **A.** Why wasn't Sophia asked to sing an encore last night?

    B. The audience wasn't pleased with her performance.
    If _____.

*come–came–come

I Wonder Why

A. I wonder why John ran by without saying hello.

B. He must have **been in a hurry**.

A. You're probably right. **If he hadn't been in a hurry, he wouldn't have run by without saying hello.**

1. I wonder why Gregory arrived late for work.
miss the bus

2. I wonder why Mario was absent from English class all last week.
be very sick

3. I wonder why Betty quit.
find a better job

4. I wonder why Rover got sick last night.
eat something he shouldn't have

5. I wonder why the apple pie tasted so fresh.

   be baked this morning

6. I wonder why Mom went to sleep so early.

   have a hard day at the office

7. I wonder why Helen prepared so much food.

   expect a lot of people to come to her party

8. I wonder why the boss was so irritable today.

   be upset about something

9. I wonder why my cactus plant died.

   have a rare disease

10. I wonder why Eleanor went home early today.

    be feeling "under the weather"

11. I wonder why Dad got stopped by a policeman.

    be driving too fast

12. I wonder why my barber cut my hair so quickly today.

    have a lot of customers after you

10. I wonder why my shirt shrank* so much

    be 100 percent cotton

11.

*shrink–shrank–shrunk

UNEXPECTED GUESTS

Melba had a very difficult situation at her house a few days ago. Her relatives from Minneapolis arrived unexpectedly, without any advance notice whatsoever, and they wanted to stay for the weekend.

Needless to say, Melba was very upset. If she had known that her relatives from Minneapolis were going to arrive and want to stay for the weekend, she would have been prepared for their visit. She would have bought a lot of food. She would have cleaned the house. And she certainly wouldn't have invited all her daughter's friends from nursery school to come over and play.

Poor Melba! She really wishes her relatives had called in advance to say they were coming.

CHECK-UP

True, False, or Maybe?

Answer True, False, or Maybe (if the answer isn't in the story).

1. Melba lives in Minneapolis.
2. Her relatives didn't call to say they were coming.
3. If Melba had been prepared for their visit, she probably wouldn't have been upset.
4. When her relatives arrived, Melba was very upset, but she didn't say so.
5. If her house had been clean and she had had more food, Melba would have been more prepared for her relatives' unexpected visit.
6. Melba's relatives realized they should have called in advance to say they were coming.

What's the Word?

Complete these sentences using would have or wouldn't have and the correct form of the verb.

1. If the plane had arrived on time, I (be) _____ late.
2. If the weather had been nice yesterday, we (go) _____ on a picnic.
3. If I hadn't been out of town, I (miss) _____ the meeting.
4. If I had seen that "stop" sign, Officer, I certainly (drive) _____ through it.
5. If the President hadn't been in a hurry, he (give) _____ a longer speech.

How about YOU?

Have you ever had a difficult situation when something unexpected happened and you weren't prepared? Tell about it.

WISHING IT HAD HAPPENED DIFFERENTLY

Rick forgot to take his notebook home yesterday. He really wishes he had remembered it. If he had remembered it, he would have been able to study last night for today's science test. And if he had been able to study for today's science test, he probably wouldn't have done so badly on it.

Alice's alarm clock didn't ring this morning. She really wishes it had rung. If it had rung, she wouldn't have been late for work this morning. And if she hadn't been late, her supervisor wouldn't have scolded her.

Peter filled out his income tax form very quickly this year. He really wishes he had filled it out more carefully. If he had filled it out more carefully, he wouldn't have made so many mistakes. And if he hadn't made so many mistakes, he wouldn't have gotten into trouble with the Internal Revenue Service.

Mr. and Mrs. Miller didn't follow the directions on the box when they baked brownies yesterday. They really wish they had. If they had followed the directions, they would have used the right ingredients. And if they had used the right ingredients, the brownies probably wouldn't have been as hard as rocks!

✓CHECK-UP

True, False, or Maybe?

Answer True, False, or Maybe (if the answer isn't in the story).

1. Rick didn't do very well on the science test.
2. He wishes he hadn't forgotten his notebook.

3. Alice's supervisor didn't scold her.
4. If Peter hadn't completed the form quickly, he wouldn't have made any mistakes.
5. Mr. and Mrs. Miller's cookies would have been softer if they hadn't used the wrong ingredients.

Have you ever done something and then regretted it? Tell about something you wish you had done differently, and why.

How about YOU?

I Wish

I **live** in Boston.
I **wish** I **lived** in New York.

I **lived** in Boston.
I **wish** I **had lived** in New York.

I don't know my neighbors.
I'm lonely.

A. You know, I wish I knew my neighbors.

B. Oh, really? Why?

A. If I knew my neighbors, I wouldn't be lonely.

B. I know what you mean.

I didn't know how to get around the city when I moved here. I was so confused.

A. You know, I wish I had known how to get around the city when I moved here.

B. Oh, really? Why?

A. If I had known how to get around the city when I moved here, I wouldn't have been so confused.

B. I know what you mean.

1. I don't have a good memory. I forget* people's names all the time.

*forget–forgot–forgotten

2. I didn't have my shopping list with me this morning. I forgot to buy eggs.

3. I don't drive to work. I have to wait for the bus every morning.

4. I didn't drive to work today. I had to wait forty minutes for the subway.

5. I don't have a good job. I'm very concerned about my future.

6. I didn't have a flu shot last fall. I was sick all winter.

7. I don't do daily exercises. I have to go on a diet.

8. I didn't do my homework last night. I had to do my homework early this morning.

9. I'm not an optimist. I get depressed so often.

10. I wasn't prepared for my English test. I got a low grade.

11. My husband and I don't take dance lessons. We feel very "out of place" at parties.

12. I didn't take two aspirin when my tooth began to hurt. I felt miserable all day.

RUMORS

All the people at the office are talking about Samantha these days. There's a rumor that Samantha is going to get married soon, and everybody is convinced that the rumor is true. After all, if she weren't going to get married soon, she wouldn't be asking everybody about houses for sale in the area. She wouldn't have requested two weeks off next month. And she DEFINITELY wouldn't be wearing a beautiful new ring from her boyfriend!

Of course, the people at the office don't know for sure whether Samantha is going to get married soon. It's only a rumor. They'll just have to wait and see.

All the assembly-line workers at the National Motors automobile factory are worrying about the future these days. There's a rumor that the factory is going to close down soon, and everybody is convinced that the rumor is true. After all, if the factory weren't going to close down soon, everybody on the night shift wouldn't have been laid off. The managers wouldn't all be reading the want ads and working on their resumes. And the boss DEFINITELY wouldn't have canceled the annual company picnic!

Of course, the assembly-line workers at National Motors don't know for sure whether the factory is going to close down soon. It's only a rumor. They'll just have to wait and see.

 CHECK-UP

True, False, or Maybe?

Answer True, False, or Maybe (if the answer isn't in the story).

1. Samantha is going to get married soon.
2. Samantha isn't asking about houses in the area.
3. The people at the office think Samantha wouldn't have gotten a new ring if she weren't going to get married.
4. There's a rumor that workers on the night shift at the National Motors factory are going to lose their jobs.
5. There isn't going to be a company picnic this year.
6. If the rumor is true, the factory will close down soon.

IN YOUR OWN WORDS

For Writing and Discussion

Have you heard any rumors lately at school or at work? Tell a story about a rumor.

What's the rumor?
Do people think the rumor is true?
Why or why not?

CHECK-UP

Choose

1. The students in our class were upset when our teacher quit last week.
   a. We won't be upset if she doesn't quit.
   b. We wouldn't be upset if she didn't quit.
   c. We wouldn't have been upset if she hadn't quit.

2. I didn't come over to your table and have lunch with you because I didn't see you in the cafeteria.
   a. If I saw you, I would have come over and had lunch with you.
   b. If I had seen you, I would have come over and had lunch with you.
   c. If I had seen you, I would come over and have lunch with you.

3. I'm afraid I can't help you type those letters because I'm going to leave work early today.
   a. If I weren't going to leave early today, I'd help you type those letters.
   b. If I were going to leave early today, I'd help you type those letters.
   c. If I were going to leave early today, I wouldn't help you type those letters.

4. Betsy didn't bring her umbrella to work today. She got wet on the way home.
   a. If Betsy hadn't brought her umbrella to work today, she wouldn't have gotten wet.
   b. If Betsy had brought her umbrella to work today, she wouldn't have gotten wet.
   c. If Betsy hadn't brought her umbrella to work today, she would have gotten wet.

Listening

Listen and choose the statement that is true based on what you hear.

1. a. He's rich.
   b. He isn't rich.

2. a. She wrote down his phone number.
   b. She didn't write down his phone number.

3. a. He would have enjoyed the play more if he had sat in a better seat.
   b. He wouldn't have enjoyed the play more if he had sat in a better seat.

4. a. The boys in the hallway aren't the landlord's children.
   b. The boys in the hallway are the landlord's children.

5. a. He didn't get the job he applied for.
   b. He got the job he applied for.

6. a. Johnny's grandparents are at his party.
   b. Johnny's grandparents couldn't come to his party.

ON YOUR OWN: Wishes and Hopes

I hope it's sunny tomorrow.   (It might be sunny.)
I wish it were sunny.   (It isn't sunny.)
I wish it had been sunny   (It wasn't sunny.)
during our picnic.

Practice these conversations.

1.

A. I hope it's a nice day tomorrow.

B. How come?

A. If it's a nice day tomorrow, we'll be able to go to the beach.

2.

A. I wish I were taller.

B. Why?

A. If I were taller, I'd be able to reach the cookie jar.

3.

A. I wish I had saved my wedding dress.

B. Why?

A. If I had saved it, I could have given it to you for your wedding.

4.

A. I wish I had finished medical school.

B. What makes you say that?

A. If I had finished medical school, I probably would have been a very good doctor.

5.

A. I hope we don't have to go to school tomorrow.

B. I hope so, too.

A. If we don't have to go to school, we can play outside all day and build a snowman.

6.

A. I wish I didn't have to go to work tomorrow.

B. Why?

A. If I didn't have to go to work, I could watch my daughter perform in her school play.

7.

A. I wish we hadn't bought Teddy a chemistry set for his birthday.

B. How come?

A. If we hadn't bought him a chemistry set, he wouldn't have set the house on fire.

What do YOU hope? What do YOU wish? Why? Share your thoughts with other students.

GRAMMAR

Past Unreal Conditional (If—would have)

If	I he she we you they	had known their address,	I he she we you they	**would have** written to them.

If	I he she we you they	hadn't missed the bus,	I he she we you they	**wouldn't have** been late.

Wish-Clauses

I We You They	wish	I we you they	had driven to work today. hadn't forgotten to buy eggs.
He She	wishes	he she	

I live in New York. I wish I lived in California.	I lived in Boston. I wish I had lived in Miami.
I don't know my neighbors. I wish I knew my neighbors.	I didn't have a flu shot last fall. I wish I had had a flu shot last fall.

FUNCTIONS

Asking for and Reporting Information

Why?
How come?

Why *didn't Peter take his umbrella to work today?*

I wonder why *John ran by without saying hello.*

If *he had known it was going to rain, he* would have *taken his umbrella to work.*

If *he hadn't been in a hurry, he* wouldn't have *run by without saying hello.*

Responding to Information

Oh, really? Why?

Indicating Understanding

I know what you mean.

Making a Deduction

He must have *been in a hurry.*

Expressing Agreement

You're probably right.

Expressing Hope

I hope *it's a nice day tomorrow.*

Wishing

I wish *I knew my neighbors.*
I wish *I were taller.*

Expressing Ability

If it's a nice day tomorrow, we'll be able to *go to the beach.*

If I had saved it, I could have *given it to you for your wedding.*

Initiating a Topic

You know,...

Reported Speech ■
Sequence of Tenses ■

What Did He Say?

"I'm sick."
"I like jazz."
"I'm going to buy a new car."
"I went to Paris last year."   He said (that)*
"I've already seen the movie."
"I was studying."
"I'll call the doctor."
"I can help you."

he was sick.
he liked jazz.
he was going to buy a new car.
he had gone to Paris last year.
he had already seen the movie.
he had been studying.
he would call the doctor.
he could help me.

A. I forgot to tell you. Marvin called yesterday.

B. Really? What did he say?

A. He said (that)* **he thought he was falling in love with me**.

A. I forgot to tell you. _____ called yesterday.

B. Really? What did _____ say?

A. _____ said (that)* _____.

---

*Or: He told me (that)

1. Peter

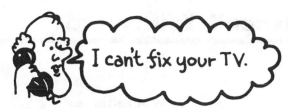

2. the TV repairman

3. our niece Patty

4. our nephew Robert

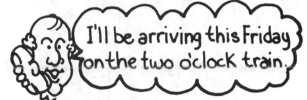

5. Uncle Charlie

6. our upstairs neighbors

7. my boss

8. Peggy and George

9. Aunt Edith

10. my boyfriend

11. the little girl down the street

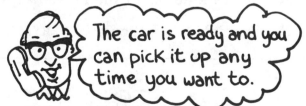

12. the auto mechanic

13. my brother

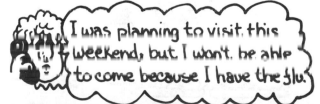

14. Grandma

Haven't You Heard?

| John **works** here. | I knew / I didn't know | (that) John **worked** here. |

A. What's everybody talking about?

B. Haven't you heard? Jack is going to be a father!

A. You're kidding! I didn't know (that) Jack was going to be a father.

B. You didn't?! I thought EVERYBODY knew (that) Jack was going to be a father!

A. What's everybody _____ about?

B. Haven't you heard? _____!

A. You're kidding! I didn't know (that) _____.

B. You didn't?! I thought EVERYBODY knew (that) _____!

1. What's everybody so upset about?

2. What's everybody talking about?

3. What's everybody so happy about?

4. What's everybody so upset about?

5. What's everybody so angry about?

6. What's everybody so nervous about?

7. What's everybody so excited about?

8. What's everybody so happy about?

9. What's everybody so excited about?

10. What's everybody talking about?

11. What's everybody so upset about?

12.

WHILE YOU WERE GONE

Dear Mom,

I'm at my friend Julie's house right now. I'll be home at five. There were a lot of phone calls this afternoon while you were gone.

The plumber called. He said he couldn't fix the bathtub because he was sick.

Grandma called. She said Grandpa was feeling much better today.

Mr. and Mrs. Davis called. They said they wouldn't be able to come to dinner this Saturday night.

The landlord called. He said he hadn't received this month's rent yet.

Cousin Sue called. She said she was sorry she hadn't had time to come over and visit last Saturday.

Uncle Harry called. He said he would call back later.

The neighbors across the street called. They said they had been robbed last night.

And finally, Joe's Auto Repair Shop called. They said they had fixed the radiator but they had found a few things wrong with the engine and it would cost an additional $200.

Love,
Sally

✓ CHECK-UP

Q & A

Sally's mother is working late at the office today. She's calling Sally to find out how things are at home. Create dialogs based on the following model and the information below.

A. Tell me, have there been any calls?
B. Yes. *The plumber* called.
A. Oh? What did *he* say?
B. *He* said *he was still sick and he couldn't come over today.*

1. Grandma: "Grandpa isn't feeling very well today and wants to call the doctor."
2. Mr. and Mrs. Davis: "Our plans have changed and we CAN come to dinner after all."
3. The landlord: "I received your check this morning."
4. Cousin Sue: "I'll be able to visit you next weekend."
5. Uncle Harry: "I'm getting married and I want all of you to come to my wedding."
6. The neighbors across the street: "The police caught the man who robbed our house."
7. Joe's Auto Repair Shop: "We've finished working on the engine, and the car is ready to be picked up."

What's the Word?

Fill in the correct words to complete the story, using the illustration as a guide.

Well,...

Your older brother got engaged.

Your sister and brother-in-law are going to have a baby.

Your younger brother was slightly hurt in a car accident.

Your father is planning to retire next month.

There was a big fire at the high school.

The shoe factory closed and two thousand people lost their jobs.

The dog had six puppies.

And your high school sweetheart married a movie star and moved to Hollywood.

Aside from that, not much else has happened.

Hi, Mom! What's new?

HOME FROM THE NAVY

Bill serves as a lieutenant in the navy. He returned home last weekend after being away at sea for several months. Since he hadn't been in touch with his family for a long time, he was very surprised at all the things that had happened while he was away.

He didn't know his older brother __*had*__ __*gotten*__ engaged. He also didn't know his sister and brother-in-law _____ _____ _____[1] have a baby. He hadn't heard that his younger brother _____ _____[2] slightly hurt in a car accident. He was unaware that his father _____ _____ _____[3] retire next month.

In addition, he didn't know there _____ _____[4] a big fire at the high school. He hadn't heard that the shoe factory _____ _____[5] and two thousand people _____ _____[6] their jobs. He also hadn't heard that the dog _____ _____[7] six puppies. And he had no idea that his high school sweetheart _____ _____[8] a movie star and _____ _____[9] to Hollywood.

A lot of things certainly had changed while Bill was away.

True, False, or Maybe?

Answer True, False, or Maybe (if the answer isn't in the story).

1. Bill has been on a ship for the past several months.
2. His sister had a baby while he was away.
3. His younger brother wasn't hurt very badly when he was in a car accident recently.
4. Bill's high school was very large.
5. Bill's former girlfriend lives in Hollywood now.

Listening

Listen and choose the statement that is true based on what you hear.

1. a. He didn't know that his supervisor had been in the hospital.
   b. He didn't know that his supervisor was in the hospital.

2. a. It's snowing.
   b. It snowed.

3. a. He wasn't aware that jackets were on sale.
   b. He didn't know jackets had been on sale.

4. a. She didn't know he had to work on Saturday.
   b. She didn't know he had worked on Saturday.

5. a. She was aware that Roger had been thinking of leaving.
   b. She was unaware that Roger had been thinking of leaving.

6. a. Her friends hadn't told her they were going to move.
   b. Her friends had told her they were going to move.

What Did They Ask?

"Where is the bank?"
"When are you going to visit me?"

"Do you speak English?"

"Have you seen Mary?"

He asked me

- where the bank was.
- when I was going to visit him.
- $\begin{Bmatrix} \text{if} \\ \text{whether} \end{Bmatrix}$ I spoke English.
- $\begin{Bmatrix} \text{if} \\ \text{whether} \end{Bmatrix}$ I had seen Mary.

A. You won't believe what a three-year-old girl asked me today!

B. What did she ask you?

A. She asked me why there was a Santa Claus in every department store in town.

B. I can't believe she asked you that!

A. I can't either.

A. You won't believe what a taxi driver asked me today!

B. What did he ask you?

A. He asked me $\begin{Bmatrix} \text{if} \\ \text{whether} \end{Bmatrix}$ I knew how to fix a flat tire.

B. I can't believe he asked you that!

A. I can't either.

A. You won't believe what _____ asked me today!

B. What did _____ ask you?

A. _____ asked me _____.

B. I can't believe _____ asked you that!

A. I can't either.

1. *my math teacher*

2. *my boyfriend*

3. *my students*

4. *the woman at my job interview*

5. *my philosophy professor*

6. *my nine-year-old nephew*

7. *my basketball coach*

8. *my daughter*

9. *my parents*

10. *my boss*

11. *my son*

12. *one of my patients*

13. *a door-to-door salesman*

14.

READING

THE JOB INTERVIEW

Charles had a job interview a few days ago at the United Insurance Company. The interview lasted almost an hour, and Charles had to answer a lot of questions.

First, the interviewer asked Charles where he had gone to school. Then, she asked if he had had any special training. She asked where he had worked. She also asked whether he was willing to move to another city. She wanted to know if he could work overtime and weekends. She asked him how his health was. She asked him whether he had ever been fired. She wanted to know why he had had four different jobs in the past year.

And finally, the interviewer asked the most difficult question. She wanted to know why Charles thought he was more qualified for the position than the other sixty-two people who had applied.

Charles had never been asked so many questions at a job interview before. He doesn't know how well he did, but he tried his best.

CHECK-UP

Q & A

You're applying for a job at the United Insurance Company. Role-play a job interview with another student, using the questions in the illustration as a guide.

How about YOU?

1. Tell about a job interview you have had.
   Where was the interview?
   How long did it last?
   What questions did the interviewer ask?
   What were your answers?
   What was the most difficult question, and how did you answer it?
   Did you get the job?

2. Job interviewers sometimes like to ask difficult questions. Why do you think they do this? What are some difficult questions interviewers might ask? Make a list and think of answers to these questions.

Why Did They Tell You That?

"Call me after five o'clock."
"Stop smoking!"

"Don't worry!"
"Don't call me before nine o'clock."

He told me
{
to call him after five o'clock.
to stop smoking.

not to worry.
not to call him before nine o'clock.
}

A. I'm a little annoyed at the mailman.

B. How come?

A. He told me to keep my dog in the house.

B. Why did he tell you that?

A. He said (that) he was afraid to deliver my mail.

A. I'm a little annoyed at my English students.

B. How come?

A. They told me not to give them any homework this weekend.

B. Why did they tell you that?

A. They said (that) they were tired of English grammar.

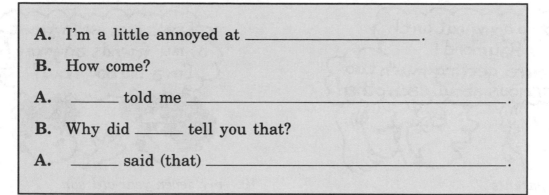

1. *my doctor*

2. *my girlfriend*

3. *the school-bus driver*

4. *my dentist*

5. *my neighbors across the hall*

6. *my teacher*

7. *my nurse*

8. *my boss*

111

9. *my parents*

10. *my seven-year-old son*

11. *my landlord*

12. *my neighbors across the street*

ON YOUR OWN: Feelings

1. **Do you remember the last time somebody said something that really annoyed you?**

   What did the person say?
   (He/She told me...)
   Why do you think he/she said that?
   Did you say anything back?

   Talk about this with other students.

2.

> "Bob would be angry if somebody told him he didn't play baseball very well."
> "Patty would be upset if her parents told her to stop watching TV."
> "Mike would be jealous if his girlfriend told him she wanted to go out with other boys."

   Do you get angry, upset or jealous very easily? Complete these sentences and discuss with other students:

   I would be angry if _____ told me _____.
   I would be upset if _____ told me _____.
   I would be jealous if _____ told me _____.

GOOD ADVICE

Margaret had a bad stomachache yesterday afternoon. She called her doctor and asked him what she should do. Her doctor told her to rest in bed. He also told her not to eat too much for dinner. And he told her to call him in the morning if she was still sick. Margaret felt better after speaking with her doctor. She's glad she can always depend on him for good advice.

Eric went out on his first date yesterday evening. Before he left the house, he asked his parents if they had any advice. They told him to be polite when he met the girl's mother and father. They also told him not to drive too fast. And they told him not to bring his date home any later than ten o'clock. Eric felt more prepared for his date after speaking with his parents. He's glad he can always depend on them for good advice.

The day before Mrs. Benson's students took their college entrance examination, they asked Mrs. Benson if she had any helpful advice. She told them to answer the questions quickly but carefully. She also told them not to get nervous. And she told them to get a good night's sleep before the test. Mrs. Benson's students felt more confident after speaking with her. They're glad they can always depend on her for good advice.

Mr. and Mrs. Newton are going away on vacation soon and are a little concerned because there have been several robberies in their neighborhood recently. They called the police and asked them what they could do to prevent their house from being broken into while they were away. The police told them to lock all the windows and leave on a few lights. They also advised them to ask the neighbors to pick up the mail. And they warned them not to tell too many people that they would be away. Mr. and Mrs. Newton felt reassured after speaking with the police. They're glad they can always depend on them for good advice.

IN YOUR OWN WORDS

For Writing and Discussion

Tell about some situations in which people have given you good advice. For each situation, answer these questions:

Why did you need advice?
Who did you ask, and what did you ask?
What did the person tell you?

GRAMMAR

Reported Speech
Sequence of Tenses

"I'm sick."	he was sick.
"I like jazz."	he liked jazz.
"I'm going to buy a new car."	he was going to buy a new car.
"I went to Paris last year."	He said (that) he had gone to Paris last year.
"I've already seen the movie."	he had already seen the movie.
"I was studying."	he had been studying.
"I'll call the doctor."	he would call the doctor.
"I can help you."	he could help me.

John works here.	I knew (that)	John worked here.
Our teacher is in the hospital.	I didn't know (that)	our teacher was in the hospital.
There's going to be a snowstorm tonight.		there was going to be a snowstorm tonight.

"Where is the bank?"		where the bank was.
"When are you going to visit me?"	He asked me	when I was going to visit him.
"Do you speak English?"		{if / whether} I spoke English.
"Have you seen Mary?"		{if / whether} I had seen Mary.

"Call me after five o'clock."		to call him after five o'clock.
"Stop smoking!"	He told me	to stop smoking.
"Don't worry!"		not to worry.
"Don't call me before nine o'clock."		not to call him before nine o'clock.

FUNCTIONS

Asking for and Reporting Information

What did *he* say?

What's everybody talking about?
  Haven't you heard?

What did *she* ask you?
  She asked me *why there was a Santa Claus in every department store in town.*

Why did *he* tell you that?

Tell me, _____?

How come?

The plumber called.
Marvin called yesterday.

He said (that) *he thought he was falling in love with me.*

He told me to *keep my dog in the house.*
They told me not to *give them any homework.*

I didn't know (that) *Jack was going to be a father.*

You won't believe *what a three-year-old girl asked me today!*

Expressing Surprise-Disbelief

You're kidding!

You didn't?!

I can't believe *she asked you that!*

Describing Feelings-Emotions

What's everybody so {upset / happy / angry / nervous / excited} about?

I'm a little angry at *the mailman.*

I would be {angry / upset / jealous} if _____.

Responding to Information

Really?

Forgetting

I forgot to *tell you.*

Tag Questions ■
Emphatic Sentences ■

This Is the Bus to the Mall, Isn't It?

John **is** here, **isn't** he? You **were** sick, **weren't** you? Maria **will** be here soon, **won't** she? Bobby **has** gone to bed, **hasn't** he?	You like ice cream, **don't** you? Henry worked yesterday, **didn't** he?

A. This is the bus to the mall, isn't it?

B. Yes, it is.

A. That's what I thought.

1. Abraham Lincoln was our sixteenth president, _____?

2. I can skate here, _____?

3. Ms. Smith will be out of town next week, _____?

4. The President is going to speak on TV tonight, _____?

5. We've already seen this movie, _____?

6. You were a waiter in the restaurant across the street, _____?

7. You live in apartment seventeen, _____?

8. You locked the front door, _____?

9. You're a famous movie star, _____?

Your Son Isn't Allergic to Penicillin, Is He?

John **isn't** here, **is** he?
You **weren't** angry, **were** you?
Sally **won't** be late, **will** she?
You **haven't** eaten, **have** you?

George **doesn't** smoke, **does** he?
They **didn't** leave, **did** they?

A. Your son isn't allergic to penicillin, is he?

B. No, he isn't.

A. That's what I thought.

1. You aren't really going to go swimming today, _____?

2. I can't have any more candy, _____?

3. The mail hasn't come yet, _____?

4. There weren't any airplanes when you were a little boy, _____?

5. Dr. Anderson won't be in the office tomorrow, _____?

6. I shouldn't take these pills right after I eat, _____?

7. The children don't ride this old bicycle any more, _____?

8. We didn't have any homework for today, _____?

9. I haven't taught "tag questions" before, _____?

I'm Really Surprised

A. You like to dance, don't you?

B. No, I don't.

A. You DON'T?! I'm really surprised! I was SURE you liked to dance!

A. This park isn't dangerous at night, is it?

B. Yes, it is.

A. It IS?! I'm really surprised! I was SURE this park wasn't dangerous at night!

1. **A.** It's going to be a nice day tomorrow, _____?

   B. No, _____.

2. **A.** The children aren't asleep yet, _____?

   B. Yes, _____.

3. **A.** This building has an elevator, _____?

   B. No, _____.

4. **A.** I don't have to wear a tie in this restaurant, _____?

   B. Yes, _____.

5. **A.** The post office hasn't closed yet, _____?

   B. Yes, _____.

6. **A.** You can swim, _____?

   B. No, _____.

7. **A.** I did well on the exam, _____?

   B. No, _____.

8. **A.** Dolphins can't talk, _____?

   B. Yes, _____.

9. **A.** The earth is flat, _____?

   B. No, _____.

10. **A.** I wasn't going over fifty-five miles per hour, _____?

    B. Yes, _____.

11. **A.** We have a spare tire, _____?

    B. No, _____.

12. **A.** You won't be offended if I don't finish your delicious cake, _____?

    B. Yes, _____.

Congratulations!

A. I have some good news!

B. What is it?

A. My wife and I are celebrating our fiftieth wedding anniversary tomorrow!

B. You ARE?!

A. Yes, we are.

B. I don't believe it! You aren't REALLY celebrating your fiftieth wedding anniversary tomorrow, are you?

A. Yes, it's true. We ARE!

B. Well, congratulations! I'm very glad to hear that!

A. I have some good news!

B. What is it?

A. I got a fifty-dollar-a-week raise!

B. You DID?!

A. Yes, I did.

B. I don't believe it! You didn't REALLY get a fifty-dollar-a-week raise, did you?

A. Yes, it's true. I DID!

B. Well, congratulations! I'm very glad to hear that!

1. I won the lottery!

2. I'm going to have a baby!

3. I've been promoted!

4. The mayor wants me to paint his portrait!

5. I'm going to be the star of the school play!

6. We've found the man who robbed your house!

7. I can tie my shoes by myself!

8. My daughter has been accepted by Harvard University!

9. We won the football championship today!

10. I was interviewed by the *New York Times* yesterday!

11. I've discovered a cure for the common cold!

12.

You're Right!

Mary is late.
George was angry.
They aren't very friendly.
I don't know the answer.

Mary IS late.
George WAS angry.
They AREN'T very friendly.
I DON'T know the answer.

They work hard.
John looks tired.
Janet came late to class.

They DO work hard.
John DOES look tired.
Janet DID come late to class.

A. You know . . . the color blue looks very good on you.

B. Come to think of it, you're right!
The color blue DOES look very good on me, doesn't it.

A. You know . . . it isn't a very good day to fly a kite.

B. Come to think of it, you're right!
It ISN'T a very good day to fly a kite, is it.

1. . . . you work too hard.

2. . . . Rover is a very talented dog.

3. . . . Uncle Frank hasn't called in a long time.

4. . . . that was an awful movie.

5. . . . this milk tastes sour.

6. . . . you have quite a few gray hairs.

7. . . . we really shouldn't be hitchhiking at night.

8. . . . Chapter 9 is easier than Chapter 8.

9. . . . little Bobby talks in much longer sentences now.

10. . . . you won't be able to play soccer for several months.

11. . . . you've been talking on the telephone for a long time.

12. . . . our English teacher gave us a lot of homework last night.

13. . . . our grandchildren don't write as often as they used to.

14. . . . the choir sang beautifully this morning.

15. . . . your brother and my sister would probably make a nice couple.

16. . . . you did your homework very carelessly.

17. . . . this new toaster doesn't work very well.

18.

A BROKEN ENGAGEMENT

Dear John,

It's been a long time since I have written to you, hasn't it. I'm sorry it has taken me such a long time to write, but I really don't know where to begin this letter. You see, John, things have been very difficult since you took that job overseas several months ago. It has been very difficult for me to be engaged to somebody who is four thousand miles away, so I have decided that things have got to change.

I have decided to move out of my parents' house.

I'm going to get my own apartment.

I have started dating other guys.

I want to break our engagement.

And I gave your mother back the ring you had given me.

I'm sorry things have to end this way. You <u>DO</u> understand why I must do this, don't you?

Sincerely,
Jane

Dear Jane,

I received your letter today and I couldn't believe what you had written.

You haven't really decided to move out of your parents' house, have you?

You aren't really going to get your own apartment, are you?

You haven't really started dating other guys, have you?

You don't really want to break our engagement, do you?

And you didn't really give my mother back the ring I had given you, did you?

Please answer me as soon as possible!

Love,
John

P.S. You DO still love me, don't you?

Dear John,

    I HAVE decided to move out of my parents' house.
    I AM going to get my own apartment.
    I HAVE started dating other guys.
    I DO want to break our engagement.
    And I DID give your mother back the ring you had given me.
    I know this must hurt, but I DO have to be honest with you, don't I. I hope that someday you will understand.

                  Good-bye,
                  Jane

✔CHECK-UP

Answer These Questions

1. Why did Jane decide to break her engagement to John?
2. Where has Jane been living?
3. What had Jane done with the ring that John had given her?
4. How did John feel when he received Jane's first letter?
5. Did Jane realize how John would feel when he received her second letter?

Choose

1. John wanted to know if Jane _____ to break their engagement.
   a. had really decided
   b. has really decided

2. John asked Jane whether she _____ her own apartment.
   a. had really gotten
   b. was really going to get

3. In her first letter, Jane said she _____ break their engagement.
   a. wants to
   b. wanted to

4. John was hoping she _____ him.
   a. still loved
   b. had still loved

5. In Jane's second letter, she told John she really _____ to move out of her parents' house.
   a. has decided
   b. had decided

6. She told him she hoped that someday he _____.
   a. would have understood
   b. would understand

IN YOUR OWN WORDS

For Writing and Discussion

John is willing to do anything he can to save his relationship with Jane. He has some ideas about how to do this, and he's going to write to her one more time. Write John's letter to Jane.

UNFAIR ACCUSATIONS

```
To: Michael Parker
From: Ms. Lewis
Re: Your Performance at Work

I'm concerned about your performance at work.

    You have been working too slowly.

    You often get to work late.

    You took too many sick days last month.

    You aren't very polite to the customers.

    And you don't get along well with the other employees.

I'd like to meet with you as soon as possible to discuss this.
```

Michael's boss, Ms. Lewis, sent him a memo recently about his performance at work. In the memo, she said he had been working too slowly. She also said that he often got to work late. In addition, she observed that he had taken too many sick days the month before. She also mentioned that he wasn't very polite to the customers. And finally, she complained that he didn't get along well with the other employees.

When Michael got the memo, he was very upset. He feels that his boss is making unfair accusations. Michael feels that he HASN'T been working too slowly. He also feels that he DOESN'T often get to work late. In Michael's opinion, he DIDN'T take too many sick days last month. He thinks he IS polite to the customers. And he maintains that he DOES get along well with the other employees.

Michael realizes that he and his boss see things VERY differently, and he plans to speak to her about this as soon as possible.

✓ CHECK-UP

Match

Match the descriptions of job performance on the left with their meanings.

_____ 1. efficient   a. pleasant and outgoing

_____ 2. honest   b. easy to work with

_____ 3. punctual   c. works quickly and accurately

_____ 4. industrious   d. thoughtful of others

_____ 5. cooperative   e. tells the truth

_____ 6. friendly   f. does things on time

_____ 7. considerate   g. cares about the work

_____ 8. dedicated   h. works hard

Listening

Listen and decide who is speaking.

1. a. tenant–tenant
   b. tenant–mailman

2. a. student–student
   b. student–teacher

3. a. salesperson–customer
   b. wife–husband

4. a. employee–employee
   b. student–student

5. a. passenger–driver
   b. police officer–driver

6. a. doctor–nurse
   b. doctor–patient

IN YOUR OWN WORDS

For Writing and Discussion

```
              MEMO

To:
From:
Re:
```

Mr. Hopper is very pleased with Helen Baxter's performance at work. Using the story below as a guide, write a memo from Mr. Hopper to Helen Baxter.

POSITIVE FEEDBACK

Helen Baxter's boss, Mr. Hopper, sent her a memo recently about her job performance. He said that he was very pleased with her performance at work. He mentioned that she was very efficient and industrious. He observed that she got along well with her co-workers and customers. And he also said that she was very cooperative and considerate. Mr. Hopper wrote that the company had been so pleased with her work that they were going to give her a big raise.

He's She's } late, isn't { It's	he. she. it.	We're You're } late, aren't { They're	we. you. they.	I'm late, aren't I.

A. You're tired, aren't you.

B. Tired? What makes you think I'm tired?

A. Well, you're falling asleep at the wheel.

B. Now that you mention it, I guess I AM falling asleep at the wheel, aren't I.

A. You're nervous, aren't you.

B. Nervous? What makes you think I'm nervous?

A. Well, you haven't stopped pacing back and forth since early this morning.

B. Now that you mention it, I guess I HAVEN'T stopped pacing back and forth, have I.

A. You're in a bad mood, aren't you.

B. In a bad mood? What makes you think I'm in a bad mood?

A. Well, you shouted at me for no reason.

B. Now that you mention it, I guess I DID shout at you for no reason, didn't I.

A. You're _____, aren't you.

B. _____? What makes you think I'm _____?

A. Well, _____.

B. Now that you mention it, I guess _____, _____ _____.

Complete these conversations and try them with other students.

1. *nervous*

2. *angry*

3. *upset*

4. *bored*

5. *embarrassed*

6. *jealous*

129

GRAMMAR

Tag Questions

John **is** here, **isn't** he? You **were** sick, **weren't** you? Maria **will** be here soon, **won't** she? Bobby **has** gone to bed, **hasn't** he? You like ice cream, **don't** you? Henry worked yesterday, **didn't** he?	John **isn't** here, **is** he? You **weren't** sick, **were** you? Maria **won't** be late, **will** she? Bobby **hasn't** gone to bed, **has** he? You **don't** like ice cream, **do** you? Henry **didn't** work yesterday, **did** he?

I'm We're You're They're	late,	aren't	I. we. you. they.
He's She's It's		isn't	he. she. it.

Emphatic Sentences

Mary is late. George was angry. They aren't very friendly. I don't know the answer. They work hard. John looks tired. Janet came late to class.	Mary IS late. George WAS angry. They AREN'T very friendly. I DON'T know the answer. They DO work hard. John DOES look tired. Janet DID come late to class.

FUNCTIONS

Asking for and Reporting Information

This is the bus to the mall, isn't it?
You live in apartment seventeen, don't you?

Your son isn't allergic to penicillin, is he?
The children don't ride this old bicycle any more, do they?

You didn't REALLY *get a fifty-dollar-a-week raise,* did you?

What makes you think *I'm tired?*

Expressing Surprise-Disbelief

I'm really surprised!

I don't believe it!

You DON'T?!

Expressing Agreement

Come to think of it, you're right!

Now that you mention it, I guess *I AM falling asleep at the wheel, aren't I.*

Initiating a Topic

I have some good news!

You know, . . .

Congratulating

Well, congratulations! I'm very glad to hear that.

Review:
Verb Tenses ■
Conditionals ■
Gerunds ■

Would You Like to Go on a Picnic with Me Today?

A. Would you like to **go on a picnic** with me today?

B. I don't think so. To be honest, I really don't feel like **going on a picnic** today. I **went on a picnic** yesterday.

A. That's too bad. I'm really disappointed.

B. I hope you understand. If I hadn't **gone on a picnic** yesterday, I'd be VERY happy to **go on a picnic** with you today.

A. OF COURSE I understand! After all, I suppose you'd get tired of **going on picnics** if you **went on picnics** all the time!

A. Would you like to _____ with me today?

B. I don't think so. To be honest, I really don't feel like _____ing today. I _____ yesterday.

A. That's too bad. I'm really disappointed.

B. I hope you understand. If I hadn't _____ yesterday, I'd be VERY happy to _____ with you today.

A. OF COURSE I understand! After all, I suppose you'd get tired of _____ing if you _____ all the time!

1. *play baseball*

2. *see a movie*

3. *go dancing*

4. *work out at the gym*

5. *eat at a restaurant*

6. *drive around town*

7. *study Algebra*

8. *go shopping*

9. *take a walk in the park*

10.

Do You Realize What You Just Did?!

A. Do you realize what you just did?!

B. No. What did I just do?

A. You just **ate both our salads**!

B. I did?

A. Yes. You did.

B. I'm really sorry. I must have **been very hungry**.
If I hadn't **been very hungry**, I NEVER would have **eaten both our salads**!

1. *drive past my house*
   forget your address

2. *step on my feet*
   lose my balance

3. *go through a red light*
   be daydreaming

4. *hit me with your umbrella*
   be looking the other way

5. *paint the living room window*
   have my mind on something else

6. *call me Gloria*
   be thinking about somebody else

7. *drink all the milk in the refrigerator*
   be really thirsty

8. *throw out my homework*
   think it was scrap paper

9. *put my pen in your pocket*
   think it was mine

10. *put tomatoes in the onion soup*
    misunderstand the recipe

11. *give Mr. Smith's medicine to*
    Mr. Jones
    mix up Mr. Jones and Mr. Smith

12. *sit on my cat*
    think it was a pillow

A BAD DAY

Marcia made several bad decisions yesterday.

She decided to drive to work, but she should have taken the train. If she had taken the train, she wouldn't have gotten stuck in a terrible traffic jam.

She decided to have lunch with a friend at a small restaurant far from her office, but she should have gone to a place nearby. If she had gone to a place nearby, she wouldn't have been an hour late for an important afternoon appointment.

She decided not to take the garbage out until after she got home from work that evening, but she should have taken it out in the morning. If she had taken it out in the morning, her cat wouldn't have tipped over the garbage pail and made such a mess all over the kitchen.

And finally, that evening she decided to stay up late and watch a scary movie on TV, but she should have turned off the TV and gone to sleep. If she had turned off the TV and gone to sleep, she wouldn't have had terrible nightmares all night.

Marcia certainly didn't have a very good day yesterday. As a matter of fact, she probably shouldn't even have gotten out of bed in the first place. If she hadn't gotten out of bed in the first place, none of this would have ever happened!

True, False, or Maybe?

Answer True, False, or Maybe (if the answer isn't in the story).

1. Marcia probably wishes she had taken the train to work yesterday.
2. If Marcia hadn't had lunch far from her office, she would have been on time for her appointment.
3. There aren't any small restaurants near Marcia's office.
4. She decided not to take the garbage out in the morning.
5. If there hadn't been a scary movie on TV, Marcia would have gone to sleep.

How about YOU?

Listening

Listen and choose where the conversation is taking place.

1. a. department store
   b. laundromat
2. a. restaurant
   b. someone's home
3. a. bus
   b. movie theater
4. a. supermarket
   b. cafeteria
5. a. shopping mall
   b. park
6. a. airplane
   b. concert

We all sometimes make decisions we later wish we hadn't made. Tell about some bad decisions you have made over the years.
 What did you decide to do?
 What should you have done?
 Why?

Choose

1. If I ____ you were going to be in town, I would have invited you to stay at our house.
   a. knew
   b. had known

2. If ____ busy tonight, I'll call you.
   a. I weren't
   b. I'm not

3. If I ____ the plane, I probably would have gotten there faster.
   a. had taken
   b. took

4. I ____ happy to go skiing with you if you asked me.
   a. would be
   b. would have been

5. If I were you, I ____ that movie.
   a. wouldn't see
   b. would have seen

6. I wish I ____ when I was young.
   a. learned to swim
   b. had learned to swim

7. If I had been more careful, I ____ driven through that stop sign.
   a. would have
   b. wouldn't have

8. I think anybody would get tired of eating in restaurants if they ____ in restaurants all the time.
   a. eat
   b. ate

You Seem Upset. Is Anything Wrong?

A. You seem upset. Is anything wrong?

B. Yes. **The heating system in my building is broken.**

A. I'm sorry to hear that. How long **has it been broken**?

B. For **two days**.

A. I know how upset you must be. I remember when **the heating system in MY building was broken**. Is there anything I can do to help?

B. Not really. But thanks for your concern.

A. You seem upset. Is anything wrong?

B. Yes. _____.

A. I'm sorry to hear that. How long _____?

B. (For/Since) _____.

A. I know how upset you must be. I remember when

_____.

Is there anything I can do to help?

B. Not really. But thanks for your concern.

1. My best friend is angry at me.

2. My father is in the hospital.

3. My TV is broken.

4. My girlfriend wants to break up with me.

5. I'm unemployed.

6. The elevator in my apartment building is out of order.

7. I'm having trouble sleeping at night.

8. My landlord refuses to fix my bathtub.

9. My dog is lost.

10. My wisdom teeth hurt.

11. I have cockroaches in my apartment.

12. I'm having trouble communicating with my teenage daughter.

Could You Possibly Come Over and Give Me a Hand?

A. Hello, Bob? This is Sam.

B. Hi, Sam. How are you?

A. I'm okay. Listen, Bob, . . . I'm having trouble **putting in my air conditioner.** Could you possibly come over and give me a hand?

B. I'm really sorry, Sam. I'm afraid I can't come over right now. **My relatives are visiting from Chicago.** If **my relatives weren't visiting from Chicago,** I'd be GLAD to help you **put it in.**

A. Don't worry about it. If I had known **your relatives were visiting from Chicago,** I wouldn't have called you in the first place!

A. Hello, _____? This is _____.

B. Hi, _____. How are you?

A. I'm okay. Listen, _____, . . . I'm having trouble _____ing. Could you possibly come over and give me a hand?

B. I'm really sorry, _____. I'm afraid I can't come over right now.

_____.

If _____, I'd be GLAD to help you _____.

A. Don't worry about it. If I had known _____,
I wouldn't have called you in the first place!

1. *fill out an application
   for a bank loan*
   "Both my children are
   home sick today."

2. *fix my stove*
   "I have a bad cold."

3. *move my piano*
   "I have to wait for the plumber."

4. *figure out our math homework*
   "I have to help my parents clean
   our apartment."

5. *repair my bedroom window*
   "My boss and her husband
   are coming for dinner."

6. *find one of my contact lenses*
   "I'm on my way to church."

7. *pick out new wallpaper
   for my kitchen*
   "I have to take care of my
   neighbor's daughter."

8. *hook up my VCR**
   "I'm late for a job interview."

9. *replace the cold water faucet
   in my bathroom sink*
   "I'm just about to take my wife
   to the hospital."

10.

*Videocassette recorder.

Several years ago, my friends urged me not to quit my job at the post office. They told me that if I quit my job there, I would never find a better one.

I didn't follow their advice . . . and I'm glad that I didn't. I decided to quit my job at the post office, and found work as a chef in a restaurant downtown. I saved all my money for several years, and then opened a small restaurant of my own. Now my restaurant is famous, and people from all over town come to eat here.

I'm glad I didn't listen to my friends' advice. If I had listened to their advice, I probably never would have opened this restaurant and become such a success.

My brother thought I was crazy when I bought this car. He told me that if I bought this car, I'd probably have lots of problems with it.

I didn't follow his advice . . . and I'm really sorry I didn't. Since I bought this car two months ago, I've had to take it to the garage for repairs seven times.

I wish I had listened to my brother. If I had listened to him, I never would have bought such a "lemon"!

My ski instructor insisted that I was ready to try skiing down the mountain. I told him that I was really scared and that I thought I needed much more practice. He told me I was worrying too much, and that skiing down the mountain wasn't very dangerous.

I decided to take his advice. I began to ski down the mountain, but after a few seconds, I lost my balance and crashed into a tree.

I wish I hadn't listened to my ski instructor. If I hadn't listened to him, I wouldn't be lying here in the hospital with my leg in a cast.

Do you remember a time when you had to make an important decision and people gave you lots of advice?

Talk with other students about the advice people gave you and the decision you made:

What did people tell you?
Why did they tell you that?
Did you follow their advice?
What happened?
Do you think you made the right decision? Why or why not?

GRAMMAR

Verb Tenses: Review

Present Tense: To Be

> The heating system in my building **is** broken.

Present Continuous

> **I'm** having trouble putting in my air conditioner.

Simple Present

> I don't feel like going on a picnic today.

Simple Past

> You just **ate** both our salads!

Present Perfect

> How long **has** it **been** broken?
> It's **been** broken for two days.

Conditionals: Review

> **If** I hadn't gone yesterday, **I'd** be very happy to go with you today.
> **If** I hadn't been very hungry, I NEVER **would have** eaten both our salads!
> **If** I had known your relatives were visiting, I **wouldn't have** called you.

Gerunds: Review

> I don't feel like **going** on a picnic today.
> I suppose you'd get tired of **going** on picnics if you went on picnics all the time!

FUNCTIONS

Extending an Invitation

Would you like to *go on a picnic* with me *today?*

Declining an Invitation

I don't think so.

To be honest, I really don't feel like *going on a picnic today.*

I hope you understand.

If I hadn't *gone on a picnic yesterday,* I'd be VERY happy to *go on a picnic with you today.*

Expressing Disappointment

That's too bad.

I'm really disappointed.

Asking for and Reporting Information

Do you realize *what you just did?!*

How long *has it been broken?*

Apologizing

I'm really sorry.
I'm really sorry, *Sam.*

Making a Deduction

I must have *been very hungry.*

Initiating a Topic

You seem upset. Is anything wrong?

Offering to Help

Is there anything I can do to help?

Sympathizing

I'm sorry to hear that.

I know how upset you must be.

Remembering

I remember when *the heating system in MY building was broken.*

Expressing Gratitude

Thanks for *your concern.*

Greeting People

Hello, *Bob?* This is *Sam.*
 Hi, *Sam.* How are you?
I'm okay.

Focusing Attention

Listen, *Bob,...*

Requesting

Could you possibly *come over and give me a hand?*

Expressing Inability

I'm afraid I can't *come over right now.*

Making a Deduction

I suppose *you'd get tired of going on picnics if you went on picnics all the time!*

Focusing Attention

After all,...

APPENDIX

Irregular Verbs

be	was	been	leave	left	left
become	became	become	lend	lent	lent
begin	began	begun	let	let	let
bite	bit	bitten	light	lit	lit
blow	blew	blown	lose	lost	lost
break	broke	broken	make	made	made
bring	brought	brought	mean	meant	meant
build	built	built	meet	met	met
buy	bought	bought	put	put	put
catch	caught	caught	quit	quit	quit
choose	chose	chosen	read	read	read
come	came	come	ride	rode	ridden
cost	cost	cost	ring	rang	rung
cut	cut	cut	run	ran	run
do	did	done	say	said	said
draw	drew	drawn	see	saw	seen
drink	drank	drunk	sell	sold	sold
drive	drove	driven	send	sent	sent
eat	ate	eaten	set	set	set
fall	fell	fallen	sew	sewed	sewed/sewn
feed	fed	fed	shake	shook	shaken
feel	felt	felt	shrink	shrank	shrunk
fight	fought	fought	sing	sang	sung
find	found	found	sit	sat	sat
fit	fit	fit	sleep	slept	slept
fly	flew	flown	speak	spoke	spoken
forget	forgot	forgotten	spend	spent	spent
forgive	forgave	forgiven	stand	stood	stood
freeze	froze	frozen	steal	stole	stolen
get	got	gotten	sweep	swept	swept
give	gave	given	swim	swam	swum
go	went	gone	take	took	taken
grow	grew	grown	teach	taught	taught
hang	hung	hung	tell	told	told
have	had	had	think	thought	thought
hear	heard	heard	throw	threw	thrown
hide	hid	hidden	understand	understood	understood
hit	hit	hit	wake	woke	woken
hold	held	held	wear	wore	worn
hurt	hurt	hurt	win	won	won
keep	kept	kept	wind	wound	wound
know	knew	known	write	wrote	written
lead	led	led			

Tape Scripts for Listening Exercises

Chapter 1 – p. 12

Listen and choose the best line to continue the conversation.

1. The dishes haven't been done yet.
2. The packages have been sent.
3. Our cat was bitten by our dog.
4. Sally was invited to John's birthday party.
5. Mrs. Brown hired Mr. Simon as a secretary.
6. Mrs. Davis was hired by Ms. Clark as a computer programmer.
7. Hello. This is Betty's Repair Shop. Your TV has been repaired.
8. Hello. This is Joe's Auto Repair Shop. I'm sorry. We've been very busy. I'm calling to tell you your car is finally being repaired.

Chapter 2 – p. 23

Listen and choose what the people are talking about.

1. A. You really should try it. You'll feel much slimmer and more energetic in just a few days.
   B. Really? I think I WILL try it.
2. A. He's looking healthier and working faster than he ever has before.
   B. You're right. I've noticed that, too.
3. A. New ones are more reliable than used ones.
   B. That's true. They are.
4. A. Here! Take as many as you want!
   B. Thanks. I appreciate it.
5. A. How do you like it?
   B. It's very good, but I think you used too much flour.

Chapter 3 – p. 40

Listen and choose where the conversation is taking place.

1. A. Do you know how much longer I'll have to stay here?
   B. Just a few more days.
   A. Oh, good.
2. A. Can you tell me why I was fired?
   B. Yes. Everybody in your department was laid off.
   A. Oh, I see.
3. A. Who knows how their lungs work?
   B. I do.
   A. Please tell us.
4. A. Do you by any chance know whether we'll be arriving soon?
   B. Yes. We'll be arriving in ten minutes.
   A. Thank you.
5. A. Could you please tell me if this book is on sale?
   B. Yes, it is.

Chapter 4 – p. 48

Listen and choose the best answer based on the conversation you hear.

1. A. I couldn't hear a word he said.
   B. I couldn't, either.
2. A. By the time we got to the party, everyone had left.
   B. That's too bad.
3. A. I just interviewed a young man for the bookkeeper's position.
   B. What did you think of him?
   A. Well, he was very shy and quiet, and he was wearing a T-shirt, jeans, and sneakers.
4. A. I smell smoke!
   B. Oh, no! The cookies are burning!
5. A. I was so tired last night that I slept twelve hours and was late for work this morning.
   B. Oh. I hope the boss wasn't angry.
   A. No. He wasn't.
6. A. Could you tell me how I did on the exam?
   B. Not very well, Richard.

Chapter 5 – p. 70

Listen and choose the statement that is true based on what you hear.

1. If Albert weren't afraid of the dentist's drill, he'd go to the dentist.
2. If Senator Johnson had enough money, he'd be interested in running for the presidency.
3. I'd be very happy if Mrs. Jones were my math teacher.
4. If the company's profits increase, we'll receive bonuses.
5. If I weren't allergic to trees, I'd go hiking.
6. If I didn't have to work tonight, I'd invite you to go to the movies with me.

Chapter 6 – p. 81

Listen and write the missing words.

The Burton family lives in the city, but they wish they lived in the suburbs. If they lived in the suburbs, Mrs. Burton would be able to plant a garden and grow vegetables. Mr. Burton wouldn't have to listen to the noisy city traffic all the time. Their son, Ken, would have a backyard to play in. Their daughters, Betsy and Kathy, might not have to share a room. And their cat, Tiger, would be able to go outside and roam around and play with the other cats. It would be very difficult for the Burton family to move to the suburbs now, but perhaps some day they'll be able to. They certainly hope so.

Chapter 7 – p. 95

Listen and choose the statement that is true based on what you hear.

1. A. If I were rich, I'd travel around the world.
   B. Really? That sounds like fun!
2. A. Why didn't you call me?
   B. I would have called you if I hadn't forgotten to write down your phone number.
3. A. How did you enjoy the play?
   B. It was all right, but I wish I could have sat in a better seat.
4. A. Those boys are making a lot of noise in the hallway again.
   B. I know. It's terrible. If they weren't the landlord's children, I'd tell them to be quiet.
5. A. You know, I wish I had taken a computer course when I was in college.
   B. Why do you say that?
   A. If I had, I would have gotten the job I applied for.
6. A. Happy Birthday, Johnny! Now blow out the candles and make a wish.
   B. I wish Grandma and Grandpa were here for my birthday party.

Chapter 8 – p. 105

Listen and choose the statement that is true based on what you hear.

1. A. Have you heard the news?
   B. No. What?
   A. Our supervisor is in the hospital.
   A. Oh. I didn't know that. That's too bad.
2. A. I've been in the office all day. I wasn't aware that it had snowed.
   B. I wasn't, either.
3. A. Do you know about our special sale?
   B. No, I don't.
   A. You can buy two jackets for the price of one this week.
   B. No kidding! That's great!
4. A. Hello.
   B. Hello, Barbara? This is Jim. I'm afraid I won't be able to have dinner with you on Saturday. I have to work.
   A. Oh. That's too bad.
5. A. Roger quit his job!
   B. Really? What a surprise!
6. A. We've moved!
   B. Oh. I didn't know that. Where to?
   A. The other side of town.

Chapter 9 – p. 127

Listen and decide who is speaking.

1. A. The mail isn't here yet, is it?
   B. No. Not yet.
   A. That's what I thought.
2. A. I did well on my exam, didn't I?
   B. No, you didn't.
   A. I didn't?! I'm really surprised.
3. A. You know . . . That suit looks very good on you.
   B. Come to think of it, you're right! It DOES look very good on me, doesn't it.
   A. Yes, it does. I wonder if it's on sale.
   B. Let's ask somebody.
4. A. You've received our supervisor's memo, haven't you?
   B. Yes, I have.
5. A. You were driving over seventy miles per hour, weren't you?
   B. I guess I was. Are you going to give me a ticket?
6. A. I have some good news!
   B. What is it?
   A. You're fine. You can go home tomorrow.
   B. I CAN?!
   A. Yes. You CAN.
   B. I'm very glad to hear that.

Chapter 10 – p. 137

Listen and choose where the conversation is taking place.

1. A. Excuse me. You just put my shirts in your machine.
   B. I did?
   A. Yes, you did.
   B. I'm really sorry. I must have thought they were mine.
2. A. Do you realize what you just did?
   B. No. What did I just do?
   A. You put too much pepper in the soup. Our guests will be sneezing all night.
   B. Oh. I'm sorry. I must have been daydreaming.
3. A. I'm sorry. I must have thought this seat was mine.
   B. That's okay. Don't worry about it. I'm getting off soon anyway.
4. A. What are you going to have?
   B. I'm not sure. If I hadn't had the chicken every day last week, I'd have the chicken.
5. A. You know, I really don't feel like shopping today. Could we go someplace else and take a walk?
   B. Sure. That's fine with me.
6. A. If I had known this was going to be so boring, I wouldn't have bought a ticket.
   B. I agree. I wouldn't have bought one, either.

Glossary

The number after each word indicates the page where the word first appears. Words introduced in Books 1, 2, and 3 are not included in this list.
(adj) = adjective, (adv) = adverb, (n) = noun, (v) = verb

A

accounting **9**
accusation **126**
additional **104**
adjust **12**
admissions office **41**
advance **90**
advance notice **90**
aerobics class **23**
aggressive **66**
air **29**
ambulance **7**
answer (v) **37**
anxious **40**
anymore **64**
apology **54**
architect **13**
architecture **13**
area **94**
armchair **25**
around the house **80**
arrest (v) **7**
article **2**
as long as **77**
asleep **118**
assassinate **37**
assembly-line worker **94**
at sea **105**
attack (v) **14**
attention **12**
auto mechanic **101**
auto repair shop **10**
aware **12**

B

baby food **78**
back and forth **128**
backyard **81**
bad dream **49**
balance (n) **134**
Bangkok **9**
bank loan **141**
bank robber **33**
baseball stadium **81**
battery **12**
bee **8**
birthday present **87**
birthmark **42**
blow up **53**
bonus **64**
book store **81**

Boston Marathon **53**
brave (adj) **56**
break *our* engagement **124**
break out **13**
break up **61**
breathe **29**
bride **103**
brownie **91**
bus driver **39**
by any chance **34**

C

cactus plant **89**
cafe **21**
call (n) **104**
campaign (n) **70**
capital **37**
capture **14**
car keys **36**
carve **5**
cast (n) **143**
cause (v) **56**
cause an accident **56**
century **13**
chain (v) **56**
challenging (adj) **29**
championship **121**
characteristic (n) **42**
charge **12**
chase **51**
check (n) **104**
check with **35**
chemistry set **97**
choke (v) **71**
choose **7**
church bells **4**
Civil War **37**
clip (v) **11**
clog (v) **112**
close (v) **14**
close down **94**
closed (adj) **64**
coin **64**
college entrance examination **113**
come by **10**
come to visit **79**
commercial (n) **70**
common cold **121**
communicate **139**
company picnic **94**
complete (v) **13**
concentrate (v) **80**

concern (n) **138**
concert ticket **36**
condition (n) **12**
confident **12**
congratulations **120**
congressmen **67**
conquer **14**
considerate **25**
construction company **13**
contact lens **141**
contract (n) **7**
convinced (adj) **94**
cookie jar **96**
cooperation **22**
cooperative (adj) **127**
cotton **89**
could have **52**
couple (n) **123**
crazy **3**
cure (n) **121**
curious **57**
customer **89**

D

Dad **74**
dangerous **118**
date (v) **124**
daydream (v) **56**
deaf **39**
Declaration of Independence **37**
depend (on) **113**
design (v) **3**
destroy **13**
details **36**
die **89**
direct (v) **3**
discotheque **29**
discover **14**
disease **89**
do badly **91**
do the dishes **5**
do tricks **23**
doctor's appointment **57**
dog obedience class **23**
dolphin **119**
door-to-door salesman **108**
dream (n) **49**
dressed up (adj) **69**
drill (n) **70**
driving test **46**
drop in **64**
drop out **75**

INDEX